COMPOSING TEMPLE SUNRISE:

Overcoming Writer's Block at Burning Man

By Hassan El-Tayyab

Poetic Matrix Press

Poetic Matrix Press
John Peterson, Publisher
www.poeticmatrix.com

Acknowledgement

Thanks to:

Front and back cover art by Alice Guo

Cover design by Melody Shirazi and John Peterson

Photos in the book that were turned into sketches by
Hassan El-Tayyab and Gretjen Helene

Sketches by Stephanie Wong

Introduction by Jess Hobbs

Transcription of Temple Sunrise by Colin Sapp

Back Cover Photo by Amal Dar Aziz

Edited by Faith Adiele, Marisa Belger, David Colin Carr,
and Kayli De Saussure.

Arabic translation assistance by Devon Peterson.

For a FREE download of the Temple Sunrise song go to:
www.composingtemplesunrise.com

Contents

"The best way out is always through." -Robert Frost

COMPOSING TEMPLE SUNRISE:

Foreword

By Jess Hobbs, Co-Founder of the Flux Foundation; project co-leader Fishbug, 2010 Burning Man Temple, Zoa.

I met Hassan the day he 'happened' into to our artspace and started creating with us. We were in the final few weeks crunch-time to finish, Fishbug, our interactive sculpture that was bound for the Burning Man Arts Festival in 2009. I remember seeing him that day and leaning over to the person next to me and asking "who's the new guy." They replied, "Oh that's Hassan he showed up today and just jumped in," – like he belonged there all along – a familiar stranger. Obviously there is more to the story as you will see, but this abbreviated version reveals a great deal about Hassan. He was at a point in his life, a cross-road, where he might have chosen to give up, but instead he risked following an unknown path.

"All growth is a leap in the dark, a spontaneous unpremeditated act without benefit of experience." –Henry Miller

We all have these unknown paths in our lives, some good, some bad, but what makes us take the leap of faith to follow one? Especially one that is closer to our heart which can feel like a riskier pursuit. What pushes us over the edge to follow a dream? What is the process one must go through to open up to greater personal possibilities? Maybe one of the catalysts is to create something with others. To collaborate on a mutual goal and see it come to life. This is the process I've been witness too.

"As you navigate through the rest of your life, be open to collaboration. Other people and other people's ideas are often better than your own. Find a group of people who challenge and inspire you, spend a lot of time with them, and it will change your life." - Amy Poehler

There is a unique love that comes from seeing a friend blossom and achieve something they didn't think or even know was possible. It's something that I've been lucky enough have witnessed repeatedly during my time creating large-scale collaborative art. Enough times that it is important to question - what happens during collaboration that opens up this possibility of personal growth and evolution? There has to be something in the process of building and making together that creates the possibility to see greater things about oneself. When we build or create alone it is a wonderful thing. When we build and create together we create something beyond what an individual can do and that process of seeing your contribution to the whole connects with something in our human psyche that opens us up to greater possibilities within ourselves.

Luckily Hassan's story is not entirely unique and that's a good thing. Yes, the path he took is unique to him, but his story has echoes of others who have had a similar experience - when we create something meaningful together often our hearts and minds are opened up. Sometimes they are busted wide open, sometimes just a little crack, but either way a greater sense of self finds its way in.

"I think it is in collaboration that the nature of art is revealed."
- Steve Lacy

Dedication

To all the amazing people I've met,

and continue to meet, on this journey.

Prologue

"All that we see or seem, is but a dream within a dream."
- Edgar Allan Poe

The wind whipped dirt and sand as I wandered through the dust storm. A presence quickened my pace against it. Each step more difficult than the last. Each gust nearly ripping me off the barren landscape. "Where am I?"

I saw a woman pounding at the letters of the typewriter in front of her. She had dark skin and dark hair, a snug black leather jacket, and goggles to protect her from the scouring sands. Her eyes never left the page as I stood watching.

"Hello!" I interrupted.

"Hold on for a while if you have time. I'm writing a story for you."

She continued to type away.

"Done!" She leaned forward looking satisfied.

She handed me the note and waved goodbye as her figure faded into the dust. The desk and the note remained. The paper faded and torn at the edge. The ink had bled and the lines were unevenly spaced, but I could still read it.

Hello Stranger. To write the book that teaches you how to wake to the dream, you must become the wanderer, slow and deliberate. Your life must become the story that is the myth within the dream. There are no words on a page here, but a book holding the logos of your life.

I shot up out of my sleeping bag in a cold sweat and rubbed my eyes. "Logos of my life," I repeated aloud.

I poked my head out of the tent to make sure I wasn't still dreaming. The landscape looked as it had when I zipped it shut a few hours earlier. Other tents still stood along the riverside, snores rumbling up from a few. Glowing embers from our fire remained inside the stone circle by the shore. The pines around us pointed towards the pristine night sky.

Confident that my hazy vision was just remnants of Rem sleep, I slipped back into my sleeping bag. "Just a dream." I yawned before closing my eyes with the strange feeling that there was something more to this dream.

Composing Temple Sunrise:

Overcoming Writer's Block at Burning Man

COMPOSING TEMPLE SUNRISE:

Chapter 1

"Faith is taking the first step even though you don't see the whole staircase." — Martin Luther King, Jr.

It was day twenty-seven of my road trip across America with Hope Rideout. I rubbed my eyes when I awoke at our campsite deep in the Mississippi back country, recalling a peculiar dream I had the night before. *The wanderer slow and deliberate. What did it mean?* I've had uncanny moments of *deja vu* all my life. When moments occur, for a split second I believe there's an order to everything. Some days I've wished the feeling lasted longer.

At that moment in my trip, I was the wanderer, nearly a month into a cross-country adventure. The journey started the day I lost my job as a special education teacher. The day I got fired. It had been only a few months prior to my departure from Boston with Hope. I entered the principal's office of Lawrence Elementary as the longest school year of my teaching career was waning. He sat in front of me with a crisply ironed shirt and a perfectly shaved emotionless face.

"As you know we are having some budget cuts this year because of the recession," explained Principal Rogers. "Every school in the district has to let a teacher go. Unfortunately, we won't be able to hire you back for next year."

My heart started pounding, and my breath grew shorter. "Why me though?" Mr. Rogers shifted in his seat. "I've spoken with some of the other teachers in your program and they mentioned your lack of initiative. I know you've had a hard year."

I felt the blood rush into my face. Four years of teaching middle school kids with special needs was over in an instant. I had been punched, kicked, drooled on, swung at with a steak knife, verbally abused, and tested in more ways than I thought possible. But my patience was a fabric stretched too thin for too long. It hurt hearing it out loud.

I let a moment pass before responding, feeling the weight of each second that ticked by sitting in the sunlit office with the blinds half down. My throat felt dry and I wasn't sure how to respond. "I've worked so hard though. I don't understand."

"Seems like you just had a hard year. I think whatever you do next you need to show more focus and initiative. Don't wait for things to always come to you."

Without another word, I left his office and took the long way back to my classroom. I didn't have the energy to argue over a job I only half wanted anyway. He was right that focusing had been hard for me that year. The week before I started teaching I had just ended a rollercoaster ride of a relationship with a bipolar woman named Maya who was lazy about taking her meds. I spent the first month of my lunch breaks at Lawrence Elementary sobbing quietly to myself in my car parked a few blocks away. When the thirty minutes were up, I wiped away my tears to head back to finish the teaching day.

Teaching Special Education I knew deep down was not my calling. The endless demands of my job were actually making me miserable. I stayed out of fear for what I thought it meant to not have a "legitimate" job. What I really wanted to do felt so far out of the realm of a normal career I was terrified of it. I only wanted to be a professional musician.

My life up until then could be characterized by loss, so losing this job seemed like a natural progression. I lost my dad when I was five. The hotel room door clicked shut behind us as Dad lay passed out and stinking of booze from another routine evening of gambling and alcohol. Mom clutched both my sister's and my hand as we scurried into the hotel lobby in terror. Dad was an addict with a capital A. When he mixed his vices, Mom became the target. He'd get angry and hit her. My mom recalls being literally scared for her life. There was no turning back when we left. The three of us were never close with him again.

I had lost every sense of home I ever had. The first house my parents had was a one-story house in Sacramento, California. An orange tree from my neighbor's yard hung over into ours. The couple who lived there let us pick the fruit right off the tree. My mom would have stayed there her whole life if things had worked out. But fate had a different plan. Dad was so in debt from gambling they couldn't afford the mortgage and we lost everything. We moved in and out of seven other apartments in only 2 years before mom left dad. Mom asked him once why he wanted to move so much. "Too many bad rememories," he replied in broken English.

We left dad and moved in with my grandparents in Plymouth, Massachusetts. They helped raise my sister Sara and me as if we were their own. Staying with them offered the first bit of stability we ever had. They passed away when I was in high school and it hurt as if I had lost my parents. But losing them also meant we lost our home too. My mother, sister, and I got forced out by an ugly inheritance dispute with my mom's siblings. The three of us were uprooted again.

Growing up in that town saved us from a lot, but during those years in Plymouth, away from Dad, were their own type of difficult. Not having a dad was hard enough, but in a town like Plymouth, being Arab got you bullied. My sister changed her name to Sara Maccaferri, which was our Italian mother's maiden name. Sara has Mediterranean features and if you didn't ask, you would never know she was an Arab. She did this to hide her identity and relationship with our father. But with a name like Hassan, my ethnicity stuck out like a sore thumb. I had no way to hide that part of my identity, though at the time I wanted to.

I lost the chance at a medically normal childhood. There is a 1 in 700 chance of being born with a bilateral cleft pallet and lip and it happened to me. When a child is born with this condition their soft and hard pallet don't grow together correctly, leaving a hole in their mouth exposing the sinus cavity and an opening in their lip. It's a condition that makes for a physically and emotionally painful childhood. I've been under the knife related to my cleft pallet just shy of ten times in the first two decades of my existence. This complicated condition has caused me a lot of heartache.

I lost the confidence I'd ever be worthy of love from someone I loved. The summer before the road trip with Hope I fell hard for Maya and lost her in a matter of a few months. When we broke up, something snapped. I lost trust that I'd ever be happy with anyone. It reaffirmed my belief that I was cursed when it came to love. Every time I tried, the situation would blow up in my face, leaving me to limp along to the next partner a little weaker than before. Loosing her was the last straw.

Maybe worst of all, I had lost faith that I'd become the person I wanted to be. I had convinced myself that I was too damaged to be happy. My only professional dream was to be a songwriter, but that meant getting up in front of people and being confident night after night. It meant getting over the writer's block that had been with me almost since I landed in Boston in 2006. It meant being confident enough to hold a good band together. It meant finding faith in myself where I had none. It meant walking into the wilderness.

Losing my job sent the whole pile crashing down. My mind from that point on was constantly clawing at defining what my purpose was in the absence of a career path. I didn't get a full night of sleep for two weeks, usually waking several times each night in the middle of an unpleasant dream. There was nothing left for me in Boston. I needed to leave. I needed to get away from everything. I needed perspective. I was broken.

*D*ay twenty-seven of the trip with Hope Rideout started with an amazing plate of scrambled eggs and a side of bacon served by Hope's friends. The eight of us sat around a smoldering fire pit as we ate. After breakfast everyone at camp grabbed swimsuits and headed up the dirt road to a nearby stream.

"Who wants to jump first?" Hope shouted as we peered off the ledge of the twenty-foot incline wondering how deep the water was. No one volunteered.

Without a word, I backed up about ten feet away and sprinted toward the edge with abandon. Butterflies swirled in my stomach as my bare feet pounded the dirt. I hurled myself into the air, I heard a gasp. Perhaps mine, perhaps anothers. None of us knew what lay beneath the water's murky surface far below. I'd be the first to find out.

From free-fall, I tucked my knees to my chest and broke through the water's skin with a slap. My knees hit mud and scattered rocks. I had barely missed a fallen tree with branches my butt, guts, and eyes might have landed on. At that moment it didn't matter to me. There was nothing left to lose.

My lungs filled to capacity once my head surfaced. Cheering erupted from the platform. It's ironic that what felt like stupidity to me, came off as bravery to them. The tree that could have killed me moments before became a slippery perch as I watched Hope jump, confident that the feat was survivable. The rest of the gang followed.

The story of meeting Hope Rideout and getting in a car with her to drive across America started the evening after I was let go from my special education job in Brookline. At the end of the day, after my chat with the principal, I walked out of the school to see kids pouring out of the front door into the sunshine. My body felt like an empty shell of a person as they raced by.

When I got back to my apartment I flipped open my laptop almost immediately and put up a Craigslist rideshare ad. It was time to leave this city for a while.

Hello adventure seeker. I am planning a road trip to California and back this summer and am looking for someone to split the gas and the drive time. I don't really have too much of a timeline. I would probably leave mid July. You would not have to stay with me the whole time. We could split up at various points along the way. You could also just hitch a ride to as far as California and hop off there. If you play music or are a music lover that would probably help us get along better during the drive. Let me know if you have any questions. – Hassan

A bunch of people got back to me, but Hope's email stuck out. Even more interesting than her response, was her name. Hope Rideout.

I am also looking to go cross-country this summer, mainly for the adventure because I've never done it. I am a 26-year-old teacher, so I have the summer off. I am not a musician myself, but I do consider music to have a central place in my life. I like all sorts – but mostly college radio/indie sort of stuff. What else – I guess I'm relatively softspoken, but I like talking with new people, being outside, and doing yoga. I am friendly and sociable but I don't need to be around people all the time...I really enjoy solitude, too. Let me know if you have any questions...look forward to seeing if this might work out. ~Hope Rideout

"You coming?" Hope called towards my direction, wringing out her auburn hair with a towel.

"I'm gonna check out this sunset." I leaned back against a tree.

"We're cooking soon, so don't take too long."

I wrapped a damp towel around my shirtless torso as she clambered over the rocks and down the path to camp. The top half of the Mississippi sky was light blue, fading into dusk as a few grey clouds glided past. The lower half was splashed in pink and orange as the sun slipped lower towards the horizon.

Gazing at the night sky revealed a piece of what I was looking for in my journey. *Beauty.* Time passed and the streaks of orange and pink had all but disappeared. Stars began to flicker. The cool night air made me shiver so I pulled my towel closer to my body, every once in a while letting go to swat a large mosquito. *Stars in a big city don't shine this bright.*

I was twenty-six, in good health had a college degree and friends who respected and cared about me. I was in the midst of our cross-country road trip with some really cool folks grilling up some great chow. There was much to be grateful for.

But sometimes it's hard to find gratitude for what's right under your nose. Worse, I felt guilty for my limited capacity for gratitude.

"Read my obituary someday." I recalled Maya's parting words. They spun in my head a year later. A part of me was still stuck in a moment in time that was almost too blurry to remember. Most of what I could remember was pain. The details lost. I don't know what we talked about, why we lingered in each other's company. All I remember we did was have sex and break up, make up and have sex again. It was a whirlwind of lust and endorphins that left me with a gaping hole in my chest as wide as anything, questioning everything I thought I was.

A lone car drove down on a nearby road. *WOOOSH.* The silver moon glowed in the darkness.

I could have applied for other education jobs, but that wasn't what I wanted. I was deferring doing what I *really* wanted.

What I really wanted was to make music. Everything else was secondary. All the answers I ever needed could be found in a good song. Music was the gateway to my heart and soul and one of the only places I felt truly connected with the world. On a basic level I have always thought that music was about harnessing the human spirit. If done right, it gave you the power to communicate directly to a person's soul. Every lifer musician has his or her own story of how they found music, but I bet most didn't choose to love it. Music chooses you.

What do you do when you aren't brave enough to go after what you want and too stubborn to gracefully quit? You just become miserable I suppose. And that's what I was. Day in day out – just plain miserable. Everyday at work teaching was a day in denial, and every note I played, wrote, or sang just tortured me more. I was stuck – a self-hating musician struggling with crippling writer's block. My rhythm was shaky and I hated my guitar playing, my lyrics, and my singing. If playing in front of people left me shaking, the thought of recording turned me to stone. Recording meant facing every truth I had ever known and some truths are harder to hear than others.

Considering my current situation, being a jobless wanderer, it seemed like the perfect moment for a career change. But making music since ending things with Maya felt near impossible. In all the heartache I somehow lost my muse too. Where music was once a place I'd go to escape from the things that were bothering me, now it had the weight of the world on it. Paying rent with music was a daunting task to think about on the best of days.

There's a reason why so few people play music professionally. Being one hundred percent self-motivated is hard. Selling yourself to an amazingly talented music scene is hard. Telling your story in front of people is hard too. And doing it while making next to no money for years till you are established was a true leap of faith. All that said, not going for it was even harder. Every excuse made the hole burn through a little deeper. I hadn't written a song in so long, I believed I couldn't.

Laughter echoed down river from the campsite. Time flies when you're lost in your own deep thoughts. I made my way down the dark riverside path toward the camp, trying to pull it together, assuming that people just don't want to hear about when you're feeling down. The moon glowed with just enough light to find my way. The smell of roasted lemon chicken lingered in the air. It was dinner time.

Chapter 2

*"When one door closes another door opens; but we so often look
so long and so regretfully upon the closed door, that we do not see
the ones which open for us."* — Alexander Graham Bell

After two thousand more miles and a month of travel
under the intense rays of Southwestern sunshine, Hope
and I finally made it to Santa Barbara, California. It was the last stop
of our trip together.

State Street was electric that night. Hope and I found out we
had landed there in the midst the city's annual fiesta week. "VIVA
LA FIESTA!" people shouted for the sake of shouting as they flowed
down the crammed sidewalks. Mariachi bands played for tips, and
vendors sold colored eggs filled with confetti to smash on friends,
strangers, crushes.

I blocked out the celebration by shutting our hotel blinds.
What I hadn't told Hope was that we could have had a place to
crash at my dad's house. He would have been upset that I didn't call
him to let him know I was in town. It had been a few years since I
last saw him, but we had stayed in contact since my parent's divorce
even if the majority of it was by phone. I didn't want to see him that
night though. I didn't want Hope to meet him. I was ashamed that
that man was my father.

"Well, I'm heading out!" Hope smiled as she put on her
ruby red lipstick for a night on the town. I watched her go from my
seat atop the burgundy sheets of the double bed. I felt bad for not

going with her as it would be our last night together, but I needed the alone time.

I rubbed my head and felt a headache set in. I wondered if my dad could feel my presence in Santa Barbara. I felt like my phone could ring at any moment with him on the other end.

"How's your mom? How is Sara?" he would ask without fail every time he called.

"They're good." I answered automatically, no matter how they were really doing. What did it matter? They didn't talk to him anyway.

*I*t had been almost twenty years since my mother had walked out on my dad. My mom and sister had spent almost fifteen of those years without any contact with him. The physical walking out happened in a hotel room not unlike the one I found myself in right then. Right before dawn, it had seemed like the whole world was sleeping except my mom, my sister and me. The room was dark as my mom furiously tossed our clothes into a suitcase by the door.

"Where are we going Mom?" I waited for a response but she was too busy to answer. "Can I wake up Dad?"

"No, he's tired honey." She zipped the suitcase shut and scooped up my three-year-old sister Sara in one arm. "Let's go." I took one last look at my intoxicated father passed out drunk on the king size bed before leaving.

Mom clicked the door shut quietly behind us and we hurried down the hall in a near jog. I watched the floor numbers of the elevator blink yellow as we descended to the lobby and then out into the parking lot. I looked out the back window of our rental car expecting to see my dad rushing to catch us. The scene was one swift nervous motion. *Why isn't Dad coming?*

Mom pulled the car into an IHop and ordered us breakfast. Sara and I chomped mouthfuls of pancakes as Mom dropped a few coins into a payphone near our table sobbing hysterically. *Why is Mom crying? Where is Dad?*

By the time my sister and I figured out what was happening we were at the airport crying *our* lungs out. In an instant, we were no longer a family.

Though my mom had protested about not wanting to live in Jordan, Dad wasn't hearing or felt that it wasn't up for negotiation. My father had bought tickets for all of us, sold most of our stuff in a yard sale, and forced my mom to quit her job. In his mind, we were moving to Jordan and that was the end of it. This was where he was born and where he wanted to start raising his family. My mom could do as she liked but Sara and I were going with him. Mom was afraid that if she went against Dad, he'd take Sara and me to Jordan and she'd never see us again.

Instead of an airline flight with all four of us traveling 7,000 miles to Amman, Jordan, it ended up being only three of us 3,000 miles to Boston, Massachusetts. Gram and Papa Mac picked us up from Logan Airport and took us to Plymouth to hide.

My dad realized what was going on and came after us on another flight later that week. He took a room at the Governor Bradford motel overlooking the waterfront. It was his launch pad for desperation. He paced the town for nine days and nights completely out of his mind hoping to get his family back. He'd call and call and call. "I love you, I love you, I love you." That was all my mom remembers him saying at first. After a while the message changed. The police delivered a restraining order to him at the hotel after he threatened to burn down my grandparent's house.

One evening my mom got a phone call from the ER saying that they were in the process of pumping my dad's stomach because he had tried to kill himself by taking a bunch of pills on a belly full of booze. My mom wouldn't go see him, forcing Dad with no choice but to leave Plymouth.

Around that time, I began to experience a strange recurring nightmare about my father that stayed with me for years. The two of us were in a black tar parking lot surrounded by what seemed like an angry mob. They circled my dad and just started beating him. In the dream my body was paralyzed. I tried to scream for help but no sound came out. I tried to reach out to help him but I couldn't do that either. The mob beat him till I woke up.

Once awake I would lie in bed sobbing to myself, thinking about my family. *Who did I love the most?* Mom and Sara were always at the top of the list. Then I started asking myself this question. *If I had to choose one family member to lose from my life, who would it be?* I thought about my mom and dad, my grandparents, my sister Sara. I lastly thought about myself. I pictured everyone in a row before me waiting for my selection. Each night after the dream, I chose to sacrifice myself to save the rest of my family.

Twenty years later Dad still believes he is the victim and that my mother is the one to blame for breaking up the family. It was her fault, or my uncles, or my grand parents or anyone but himself really. Six year old me blamed myself. Mom tells me that I was a saint for the next few years. I remember my eight-year-old pal Dan used to ask me in frustration. "How are you so good?" My mom tells me now I probably was acting out of fear, afraid to lose another parent.

My entire life I've been perplexed about how to form a relationship with someone so deeply in denial as my dad. Some questions you never get the answer to. I doubt I'll ever know the full story. Every conversation we've had since almost always references that we left him. In his eyes I'm still six years old because those are the memories he has of us.

I definitely didn't want to complicate an already complicated trip by visiting him. Writing a few thoughts in a journal by the hotel window had me as close as I wanted to be to that chapter of my past.

Chapter 3

"He who isn't busy being born is busy dying"
— Bob Dylan

That morning I said goodbye to Hope. She was heading up to Oregon and I would linger in California. This was the part of the trip I was dreading as I officially had no concrete plan. As she signaled her blinker and rolled out of the parking lot, I felt a pang of sadness. I already missed her. *Goodbye Hope.*

I drove my Chevy up the scenic Route 1 along the Pacific coast. The steep cliffs of Big Sur shot straight down to a sandy beach. The air was colder and the fog all but blocked out the sun. The engine chugged up the windy incline surrounded by thick forests and jagged rock. I stopped along an open patch overlooking a wide expanse of ocean. Scattered fishing boats drifted along at the whim of the current. I found a perch on the rock wall and let my feet dangle over the edge.

My eyes closed and I put my head in my hand, thumb and index finger on my temple. I was miserable. Too miserable to be awed by this wonderful spectacle.

The chill in the air made my muscles tense. I watched the boats glide along as white caps pulled a layer of sand off the beach into the ocean.

Thoughts of suicide tugged at me. An idea that had been in my head since I lost my job. The urge to let go and end my pain. I thought of the orange tree dangling over the fence of my backyard as a kid. I thought of the hotel room we left my dad passed out in. I thought about not having a dad around growing up. I thought about the years of painful surgeries growing up with a cleft pallet. I thought about the years of being tortured for asymmetry all through my childhood. I thought about how much of a failure I felt like walking out the doors of Lawrence Elementary after losing my job. I thought about how afraid I was every time I picked up my instrument.

One thought overwhelmed them all though. Maya's bright blue eyes burned in my mind mixing with the grey expanse of ocean in front of me. She was an illusion just like her name. Here I was again, strung out on another relationship gone badly.

We'd met at a party at the beginning of last summer a year prior. Music initially connected us – she was an aspiring cellist. We spent the evening at the party playing music for each other. The chemistry was intense. She came back to my place and we had sex. She told me before sex that she was a virgin. I asked if she wanted to stop. She shook her head.

"You just have to call me," she pleaded as we said goodbye. She confided that she'd always feared being abandoned by her first lover. In her vulnerability I didn't want to hurt her. I had taken something she could never have back. I felt obligated to make sure she felt cared for. The relationship was tipped out of balance before it began.

The events of this relationship barely mattered to be honest. Everything was sex, sex and more sex. We barely talked and I have no recollection of what we spoke about when we did. I couldn't tell you who her friends were, what she did for fun, what her aspirations were, or really anything that would give you the slightest idea what made Maya tick. We were two strangers sharing a bed for months. She'd come over in the evening and I'd wake up the next morning with a hickey on my neck. Sometimes I'd wake up alone and sometimes she'd be next to me clinging for warmth. After a while, she began breaking up with me every other encounter, which led to her crying on the phone a few days later; another blurring round of sex, sex and more sex, more crying, and another giant hickey on my neck.

There was one thing that Maya and I had in common. We were both really sad and lonely people who really just wanted to feel connected to someone. We'd even settle for a fake connection.

A short time after we began seeing one another, I'm convinced the universe sent me a sign to leave Maya. The two of us were sitting on my bed during a rainstorm listening to my favorite jazz piano album, *Ahmad Jamal, Live at the Pershing*. Ahmad Jamal played smooth and clear piano lines that bounced around the scales on top of the swingy grooves, laid down by Israel Crosby and Vernell Fournier. There was so much space in between the notes, I couldn't help but fall in. Somewhere in-between one of those chords that day, she demanded that I fuck her. I was infatuated. If I could pin point a moment when I completely opened my heart to her that was it.

In an uncanny event that same rainy summer afternoon, water literally started pouring from my ceiling right between us on my bed. The roof was over a hundred years old and needed love, but I took it as a warning. I got a chorus out of it too. *There's a hole in my heart where the rain comes in,* was the refrain. Over and over it repeated. That's all I had, a hole in my heart. Over time the rest of the verses got fleshed out and tapped into the hotel room where Mom, Sara, and I left Dad. That's the interesting thing about songwriting sometimes. When done right, the words point at parts of yourself that you may not even completely understand. The water from my relationship with Maya dripped right on to the deepest and oldest wounds I had.

I was an emotional goner at that point in the relationship though and probably would have done anything for her. I rationalized that if I stayed with her the pain would just help me grow as a person. On some level I thought I deserved the abuse.

When we did finally split it was ugly. There would be no staying in touch. The relationship was over with a capital O! "Read my obituary" ended up being the last thing I heard her say. Rather than rejoicing, all I could focus on was the hurt, and it kept on hurting, well after Maya and I broke up. A well-adjusted person may have been over it in a few months, or better yet left the situation before it devolved, but instead I plunged into a deep depression. My life became a case study on extreme rumination. It eerily reminded me of the loop my dad had been stuck in since my parents' separation almost twenty years ago.

Maya had dug a hole in my heart so deep I was having a hard time climbing out. I remembered going over pointless details about her to my friend Adam months after the split. He shook me by the shoulders, "You're spiraling man. This is not about her at all. This is about your dad." I heard his words but had no response. I understood it on an analytical level, but I didn't have a clue of how to actually fix myself or get help.

I stared over the cliff at Big Sur again. *Was this all there was for me? How do I stop this cycle?* Only one thing came to mind as I looked over the edge of Big Sur: *Jump.*

My heart rate increased and my palms started to sweat. My thoughts spun around like a maple leaf in free fall. Everything I had ever tried to make things better just shattered in my hands. Every step forward only took me back two more. Was this the step forward I had been waiting for? *Do it. Jump.*

Kik-kik-kik-kik I heard behind me. A faint *kik-kik-kik* answered from a distance. A cool breeze blew off the Pacific and I could taste the salty air on my chapped lips. The wind blew again and the noisy Red-tailed Hawk nearby shot out of the Redwood above me. I watched her soar over the edge of the ravine, her blue-gray wingspan fully stretched, effortlessly gliding through the air.

"Goodbye," I whispered closing my eyes ready to let go of the ledge. Ready to follow the Red-tailed Hawk off the edge and away from every ounce of pain I'd ever felt. *Kik-kik-kik* I heard again.

Chapter 4

"When written in Chinese the word 'crisis' is composed of two characters. One represents danger, and the other represents opportunity." — John Fitzgerald Kennedy

The things you find when you aren't looking are usually what you need to find the most. It makes you wonder if the universe is playing a game or testing what you're made of. Sometimes being right up against the edge allows you to see the edge for what it is. Having our backs against the wall forces us to make order out of the chaos. I was lost on my journey but maybe lost is where I needed to be.

*T*he hot sun crept higher in the sky, burning off the cold fog along Route 1 around noon. A clear blue sky met the Pacific horizon almost as far as I could see west. Each hillcrest was a postcard image of wild surf crashing on long stretches of beach and steep cliffs.

Over one more hill was San Francisco. Homes stacked in rows like decks of cards on top of rolling hills. Skyscrapers were modern castles stretching across the vast cityscape. I peered west at the Golden Gate Bridge draped across the bay, connecting the city to redwood forests in the Marin Headlands. Even in my depressed state I could still appreciate that this was something magical. I wondered how many people before me thought the same thing. Settlers in the gold rush hoping to strike it rich. Jack Kerouac in his travels around America more times than he could count. How many poems did Allen Ginsberg write with this view in mind? This is where dreamers come to dream. A canvas for imagination.

I cruised through to the 101 North split, through the high-rises of the Financial District and between the steel support cables of the Bay Bridge. I was headed that way because I had plans that afternoon to meet Star Simpson for lunch in Berkeley. She had responded to the same ad I put up to find Hope.

Hey Hassan! My name's Star and I totally dig the Craigslist post you wrote. I'm in Berkeley, California right now, and I'm looking for someone to help me move a couple small things back to MIT next fall — a small box of books, my blanket, etc. Would you be down? Heck, you sound pretty cool, maybe we could even meet up when you're in California! Have a good road trip. - Star

She greeted me in a pair of paint-covered overalls and a wide smile in front of an Indian restaurant along a quiet side street. Star and I had no trouble getting right into some good conversation about Jack Kerouac and cross country road tripping.

After lunch, I drove her home to see if there was enough room for her stuff in my car. I didn't mention to Star my lack of timeline. Maybe I'd be back in Boston in September, but maybe I wouldn't. I thought I'd at least oblige her request. She seemed nice enough and now was a time to be open, even to complete strangers. Whether it worked out or not, I needed to be around friendly people as I figured things out.

We rolled at a slow pace only a few blocks from the restaurant and turned left down a peculiar looking side street lined with trash and potholes. I pulled up at a long pleated steel gate surrounded by large metal containers, sporting barbed wire. The gate had the word "Shipyard" on the front in faded white paint. Atop the rust colored shipping containers stood oddly shaped sculptures and old and rusty steam-powered vehicles that looked at one time to have been functional. A twenty-foot periscope peered over the wall at us.

Unbolting the chain at the front gate, she pushed the front door open and I stepped into an unfamiliar world. My eyes widened. The place was filled with gigantic art pieces and machines that appeared to be completely impractical. It looked like a magical workshop that could have belonged behind Hogwarts Castle. I craned my neck back and observed that standing over all of us were dancing figurines atop the shipping containers they called home.

I saw a person near the front of the shop wearing a welding hood flipped down. The sound of buzzing electricity shot off in a quick burst from his welding gun as bright flashes of light and sparks made the air around us smell and taste like metal dust.

On my left I saw a gigantic 18th Century Victorian house on wagon wheels. Through a dusty window I could make out the worn wooden spokes of a ship's wheel. On its roof sat the large periscope I had seen from the street.

Next to the "Neverwas" – the oversized Victorian house/car – sat another art piece. A thirty-seven foot fire-breathing insect, which I later learned was called "Fishbug." It had bright orange and red side panels and a graceful arched tail that looked like two wings. Fishbug's head was a wire cage with two shimmering stainless steel tusks projecting from the front. I stepped inside the cavern of its belly to find a painter on a 15-foot ladder white washing bare metal along Fishbug's spine. The piece was unfinished yet gorgeous.

"Want to meet some of the artists?" Star waved to me.

She led me to the back of the shop where two artists gathered for a cigarette break. One of the artists, Rebecca, wore oil-stained coveralls that hung down to a pair of completely worn paint covered boots. She had short hair that left the two orange earplugs she wore no place to hide. Rebecca had a genuine grit to her, but was warm and welcoming.

"What are you making?" I asked.

"This stuff is all going to Burning Man in a few weeks," Rebecca replied.

"I've heard of Burning Man, but I don't know much more than that."

Rebecca smiled. "Picture tens of thousands of costumed people and huge art sculptures in the middle of a desert in Nevada."

The other artist, Kruddy, interjected. "I think about one-third of the 50,000 some odd people at Burning Man every year live in the Bay Area though, so there is a pretty heavy scene in the Bay." Kruddy was tall, thin and wore faded jeans and a blue button-down shirt. A beat up cowboy hat sat on top of his head, and a five o'clock shadow covered his chin.

"Burning Man, as far as I can tell, is absolutely unique. I know very few people who have come back from it and said flat out that they were never going again." Rebecca looked to be glowing at the edge of her seat.

Kruddy nodded in agreement as his wrinkled hand reached for the pack of cigarettes in his shirt pocket. "Burning Man creates culture. This is not an ode to yippie pop culture by any means. What happens at Burning Man trickles down into mainstream society. Big blown up pieces of fire art never existed anywhere before this festival."

Kruddy tapped his cigarette against the edge of the cauldron. "Everything is a vibration and Burning Man just creates a good open vibe. I mean this place is a total outlier in comparison to most of America. It's a phenomenal thing that creative folk even *have* a place to go in our corporate run country. I like hanging out with some of the best and brightest and most creative. That is exactly what Burning Man provides."

"What could a person expect to see out there?" I found myself literally sitting on the edge of my seat. My curiosity for this festival grew with each new story. I almost caught myself drooling. It sounded amazing. It sounded better than amazing.

Rebecca stood up to split a board in half over her knee from the scrap wood box. "I guess you see what you want to see," she responded while stoking the flames. "And just for the sheer fact that you are going to see things that you have never seen before, it will change the way you see things in general. It is a gifting community out there – a week long cashless society. Everyone is an active participant and expected to give something."

"I guess I've got my guitar," I thought to myself.

After a while I said my goodbyes and left the Shipyard. I could have listened to them talk about creativity for hours. I could see creativity in the shape of a fire-breathing monster made of steel. I couldn't remember the last time I was so excited about anything. I could almost feel some stagnant, uninspired sludge melting off my spirit.

I got in my car and took one last look at the periscope attached to the Neverwas. I could swear it had had its eye on me since I had arrived. The workshop and the community of artists I had just stumbled upon embodied something I'd never experienced. The odds of finding a place like this so soon after everything I'd been through that day made me think that landing here hadn't been by chance at all. Maybe fate steered me here away from the steep cliffs of Big Sur. Maybe something had been watching out for me after all. I knew I was at the lowest point of my life and the time had come to either end it all or make a serious change.

I paid the four-dollar toll, crossed the Bay Bridge and headed back to my crash pad for an intense all night session of Burning Man research. I tore through the text on the Burning Man website paragraph by paragraph.

I learned that a San Francisco native named Larry Harvey started Burning Man in 1986 on Baker Beach in San Francisco with only twenty people. In 1990 Burning Man moved to the Black Rock Desert in Nevada where it could spread out and handle larger crowds. By 1996 over 8,000 people attended. It's grown in population ever since and tops 50,000 people annually. Burning Man got its name from the large wooden effigy burned on the last

Saturday of the event. I kept coming across people describing Burning Man as an "experiment in community," art, "radical self-expression," and "radical self-reliance." A part of their mission statement on the Burning Man website caught my eye. "Our intention is to generate society that connects each individual to his or her creative powers." The more I learned, the more I wanted to comprehend the subculture I had stumbled upon. *Was there a place in this community for a lost artist, like me, trying to find his way?*

After researching ticket prices though, my heart sank a bit. A ticket cost $300.00. My cash supply had been running low after two long months of being on the road. The ticket was probably only half what I would need to spend on Burning Man. On top of the entrance fee, I'd need food for two weeks, water, a shade structure, goggles, breathing masks, gas to Nevada and back to wherever back was, a head lamp, an appropriate tent, and other odds and ends for desert survival. This would surely be an expensive adventure! *How would I get to Burning Man?*

I absorbed as much as my brain could take in only stopping to go to the bathroom and eat dinner. I felt in my guts that I needed something from these artists and this unique community. I couldn't stop thinking about Burning Man and all the amazing things I had seen at the Shipyard. I needed to be a part of it and I wasn't even sure what *it* was.

Chapter 5

*"Sometimes you have to play for a long time
to be able to play like yourself."* — Miles Davis

The next morning, I woke up at my pal Kevin's place
near Ocean Beach with Burning Man and Fishbug on
my mind. My guitar was lying exposed on the floor next to me. Its
light wood body was dirty around the pick guard and much of the
surface had been worn from my years of playing it. The steel strings
were dead and needed to be changed.

I strummed a familiar chord progression and hummed
incoherent English. *You and me, got no other place to be, so let's be
where we find ourselves right now.*

What's next I wondered, repeating the line a few more
times. *Does that line have anything to do with the Shipyard? What's
this about? Zen philosophy maybe? And speaking of listening, this
sounds like another song too. Is this even original? And speaking of
original, I'm hungry too… actually yes, now that I think of it, I am
very hungry!*

At that point, like so many others times before, my song had
been completely derailed. *Poor guy never had a chance,* I thought
to myself as I set my guitar down and closed my journal. My head
began to ache in frustration.

There was absolutely nothing I wanted more than to write a
good song. I didn't want any more unfinished song starts. I had
enough of those. Even one fully formed, well-crafted song with a
beginning, middle and end would have made my day. I chucked

my pen across the room at the wall and looked at my instrument with contempt. It wasn't always like this though. *Where had I gone wrong?* I sprawled out on my bed and started daydreaming about my how I started playing music.

I first got into music when I was seventeen, growing up in Plymouth, as a remedy to a nagging emptiness I always carried within me. I stopped by a local music shop one day after enrolling in a music theory class in high school. I put exactly $200.00 in ones and fives I earned working in restaurants on the music store counter. In return I got a jet black Peavey Stratocaster and a small electric amp. That may have been the first real decision I ever made. I started taking lessons at Middle Street School of Music in the heart of downtown Plymouth every week. My routine was to buy an album and learn one of the tunes off it for every lesson. My pal Joey, who knew the instrument better than me, supplemented my knowledge with power chords and riffs to Classic Rock songs.

Guitar quickly became an obsession. Practicing for four hours a day became my norm. Exploration might be a better word for it. Every new chord was this amazing discovery that inspired further exploration. I'd just play a new song until I knew it inside and out. Hours went by as I played along to recordings of my favorite classic rock albums. Jimi Page to this day is my favorite guitarist. His creativity knocks me out every time. The way he took old blues ideas and created totally fresh, original and timeless songs, has in my opinion never been matched in rock and roll since.

Music became a place I could just play and pour myself into without judgment. My self-critic was so hard at work cutting me down in other areas this became my safe haven.

Eventually, I started going to an open mic held at the La La Java Coffee House every Wednesday. The other performers were great musicians in their own right and totally supportive of what I was doing. We were a community. I was in heaven once a week.

Seeing them sing and write original songs made me want to sing and write as well.

I'll never forget the first song I wrote, *The Plymouth Song.* I was cleaning a Bounce House at Taylor Rental the power tool and party rental supply store in Pembroke, Massachusetts that also served as my summer job during college. While I probably should have been vacuuming I wrote a tune on the back of an invoice. I basically rewrote the historical narrative I was taught in school about the Pilgrims who came to Plymouth in 1620. A story every Plymouth resident knows all too well. Every line came to me with ease.

Welcome to Plymouth all you tourists
Let me tell you about the Pilgrim's story
It started in the 17th century, around 1620
Besides the Pilgrims on board, was the crew and William Bradford
All together on the Mayflower, To escape English power
They ended up in Cape Cod bay, the safe waters made them stay
That's why we are here today and not P Town
That first winter was so cold, the Pilgrims had to be bold
They stuck it out and they survived, but half of them died.

It goes on and gets more politically incorrect as the verses progress. I didn't think it was that good necessarily, but it made me laugh. I sang it proudly to my boss Ray. When I rang out the last chord he said candidly, "Hassan, you really ought to find a cute girl to sing for you. Your guitar playing is actually pretty good, but your singing sucks." Ray and I had a good chuckle, but I could tell he was serious. He really did think my singing sucked. In fact most of the staff at Taylor Rental probably thought my singing sucked too. Every so often the radio in the box truck would stop working for that very reason.

"Hey the radio's busted again." I'd say returning from a delivery. What I didn't know for a few months was that they took out the fuse because they were tired of hearing me sing along to classic rock songs. It was a running joke between the whole crew, but I didn't even mind. It *was* hilarious! The best part was I didn't care what they thought on a deep level. I was just having fun with music.

When I performed it at the open mic later that week, I had completely forgotten Ray's comment. He didn't get what I was so happy about. I had actually written my very own song. It had a beginning, a middle and end. It had chords, a melody, and I remembered the words. If I learned anything from listening to Bob Dylan it was that the words and your conviction make for a good song. With the right attitude, you can pull off a good delivery. It didn't really matter that my voice wasn't perfect.

When it was my turn in the line-up, I reluctantly steepped up to the microphone, looking out at the eager audience. I squinted my eyes in the bright stage light. My heart beat faster and faster in my chest and I began to sweat. "This one is called The Plymouth Song," I said over the mic. The entire crowd hooted and clapped.

Welcome to Plymouth all you tourists. I began to sing. Every verse gave me more and more confidence. The audience seemed to enjoy every note. I barely felt nervous at all by the time I finished.

For 3 minutes, thirty people were connected with *The Plymouth Song* as the conduit. It was possibly the most connected to life I had ever felt. I'd never felt so filled with pure joy. It was a silly song, but it wasn't a silly feeling I got while performing. For the first time, I was being heard. Something clicked that night and a seed was planted. All I wanted to do from that day forward was to write and sing more songs for as many people as would listen.

*K*evin's apartment was quiet as I sat on the floor staring at my guitar with contempt. The room looked just like it had before I attempted to write, except my instrument was on the couch instead of in my hand. I pulled off my glasses and glanced again at the nearly blank page of my moleskin journal. My head began to ache again. I rubbed my throbbing temple again with my thumb and index finger. Sitting on that couch felt much different than the days of hiding in a Bounce House at Taylor Rental with a pen and paper. *Would I ever find my muse again?*

If I was ever going to be a songwriter, I needed to not only start songs but finish them too. I thought of the folks at the Shipyard. They seemed like finishers. I had so much to learn from them.

Chapter 6

*"Opportunity is missed by most people because it is
dressed in overalls and looks like work."*
— Thomas Edison

In the midst of my despair my phone buzzed. It was
Star. "Want to come back to the shop and give us a hand
building today?" she asked me. "We sure could use the help."

"Are you a mind reader?" I jokingly asked her.

When I got to the Shipyard, I found the Fishbug crew hard
at work. With Burning Man only two weeks away it was crunch
time for the artists. I walked into Rebecca's shipping container to
get some directions.

"Thanks for coming by to help! Take some work gloves.
You're going to need them." Rebecca winked. I slipped them over
my fingers and made a fist.

Kruddy was outside the container shaping a piece of wood
and I offered to lend a hand. We cut the board and fit it to the back
of the bug and secured it to the tail with a wrench.

"What's next?" I asked. He handed me a paint roller.

The day flew by as I was given task after task, but somehow
my body didn't feel tired or run down in the slightest. All day I had
one of my favorite Grateful Dead lyrics stuck in my head. *"If you've
got a job to do you got to do it well."* I leaned into every job with as
much energy as I could put out until it was complete. There would
be no unfinished song starts at the shop that day. No job done half-

assed. Today I was part of the Fishbug crew, a crew of finishers and we were on a mission to get Fishbug ready for one of the biggest art festivals on Earth!

"Drink some water, Hassan. You're making us look bad," Rebecca joked. She forced me to take a hydration break in her container. I barely noticed that I had been working til well after midnight. Time at the Shipyard moved faster than I was used to.

"When are you guys meeting again?" I asked.

"Tomorrow at noon. I hope you can make it." She smiled, handing me a jug of water. "Got to stay hydrated!"

"Thanks for including me. I had a blast today!" I noticed a photo on the wall behind her head of a man with dark hair around his early 30s. "Who is that?"

"That's my brother." All of a sudden some of the color drained out of Rebecca. "He committed suicide a few years back."

"I'm so sorry, Rebecca." I wished I hadn't mentioned it.

Rebecca unclipped her tool belt and set it next to her. "It's ok. It is what it is. He always used to say, he wasn't meant for this world." A moment passed. "I really do hope you can make it tomorrow! You're a good worker, Hassan." She gave me a hug.

I left the shop as Rebecca wrapped a few things up before leaving herself. I felt bad for bringing up her brother. How awful must that feel to lose a loved one that way.

I thought of my moment at Big Sur and how close I came to the edge. How my family would feel wasn't on my mind at all. All I could think about was myself. My pain. Talking to Rebecca made me think about the consequences. How my mom and sister would feel if I went through with it. Would they blame themselves? How could I even consider putting my family through that kind of hell. But the pain in my heart truly did outweigh the love I experienced everyday. I didn't want to commit suicide as much as I just wanted to stop hurting.

Maybe Rebecca had a hole in *her* heart too. But she used her pain to make beautiful art. She *would* carry on. She was strong.

She was a finisher! Her life would never be a half finished song. I made a promise to myself right then. *No matter what happens, I'm going to stick around til we are done with Fishbug! This is where I belong.*

*T*he next morning I made my way back to Fishbug by 11:59am. Rebecca seemed surprised to see me. It was just the two of us there, knee deep in the middle of a huge to-do list and no time to waste.

"Want to learn how to use a dangerous tool?" she asked.

"Sure," I squeaked.

Rebecca pulled a tool-laden cart out from inside the shop and showed me the plasma cutter. I learned that a plasma cutter is a torch used to cut steel by turning inert gas into plasma. The machine operates when an electric arc is passed through compressed air, creating heat so intense it can melt steel. After a quick tutorial of how to actually use the thing, she fitted me with a facemask, gloves, a respirator, goggles, and welding sleeves. The mirror on the wall reflected back at me a stranger from a sci-fi movie.

She dragged out another cart piled high with steel pipes. Yellow hand-drawn lines on them marked where the cuts needed to be made. She asked me once more if I knew what I was doing. My answer was yes and I was left to my own devices. "Trial by fire," she said with a smile and was off. My nerves prevented me from getting the pun right away.

After connecting the grounding clamp onto the first piece of steel, I pulled the trigger of the plasma cutter. It kicked back on me for a second and then settled into my tight grip. A glowing torch lit and I hunched down close to the first piece of metal laid out on the table. Shakily, I brought the torch to the pipe and began ripping into the steel following the thin yellow paint line. It took my eyes a bit to adjust to the bright light, even through the shaded goggles.

Sweat clung to my welding sleeves and frosted the inside of my goggles; my body ached from being hunched over so long. Hours went by, but I was so wrapped up in the cutting that I barely noticed. I loved every minute of the work. And I wasn't just cutting through quarter inch mild steel tubing; I was cutting through the numbness, I was cutting through layers of stagnant sludge clogging the pores of new creative growth. I was cutting away everything holding me back from who I wanted to be. I was possessed with a determination I'd never known.

I put the torch down and looked over the work with a critical eye, I noticed rough edges. *That's embarrassing. Would she need me to redo the job?* I wheeled the cart to Rebecca to get an appraisal. She slapped my arm. "You're a natural." My sore body felt a moment of joy. "Now it's time to grind!" *Uh oh!*

*S*he clamped one of my cuts to a nearby workbench, and took a hand grinder to it. Orange sparks flew as she smoothed out the rough edges of the bent steel. She turned off the grinder, and ran her hand over the smooth surface. "Nothing to it," she said. "Now you try. By the way, this is a lot of work so don't feel like you have to do it all."

I held the grinder in my hand and flipped the 'on' switch. It kicked back in my hand as I brought it closer to the coarse steel. I dug the spinning disk into the pipe, watching the coarse edges of my plasma cutting turn into bits of metal dust and smoke. My upper body vibrated with the machine in my hands as sweat trickled from my brow and underneath my breathing mask. I pushed my earplugs deeper down my ear canal to block the deafening shriek of the grinder. I dug into the pile with every intention of finishing it all. *I'm a finisher.*

Pipe by pipe, I pulled the hand grinder back and forth over the rough curves of steel, sending sparks into the air, determined to refine what I had cut. I attacked the bits of slag with the same passion I had cut the pipe with. Through my breathing mask I could smell metal dust. I turned off the grinder and readjusted the mask in the mirror and noticed my face was blackened except for the skin colored diamond over my nose and mouth. I smiled, flipped the mask down and re-entered another trance-like state. My entire world was a hand-grinder.

Hours went by and I noticed that all the steel had been ground. I wheeled the cart out to Rebecca. She beamed at the completed job and gave me a giant hug. "You rock, Hassan!"

"What's next?" I asked.

*T*he next few days were similar, just with different jobs. I painted, cut, cleaned, ground, sawed, wrenched, taped, pasted, organized, and didn't even contemplate complaining about the long hours. It was crunch time for them, and they were happy to have some extra help. I was happy they needed it. I was happy to feel needed. The Fishbug crew made me feel more respected and appreciated than I had felt in a long time. *Maybe ever!* In return, I worked as hard as I could for as long as I could each day. I was determined to make myself a valuable crewmember. I felt responsible for Fishbug as if it were my own. Pulling fourteen-hour shifts almost every day was becoming my norm.

So much of my life up to that moment had been spent worrying about my own problems. Fishbug gave me respite from that. I was a part of something bigger than myself yet not as a cog in a machine. We were making art. After seven full days of working on the piece, I asked if I could just stay at the Shipyard to avoid wasting gas and paying the four-dollar Bay Bridge toll. Rebecca said it was the least they could do for me. My new home was on the upstairs couch at the Berkeley metal shop.

The project for me the following day was building projector boxes out of plywood for the light show inside Fishbug's brain. I worked for hours trying to get it fitted perfectly. At the scrap woodpile Jess, the Fishbug's co-lead, approached me in a pair of knee high pink work boots. Jess spent more of her time working on the business side of making big art. A job that required her to be in the office for long hours at the Shipyard. In her hand was an envelope. The word *Fishbug* was written on the front. She smiled. "Open it."

As I opened the letter I felt my heart beating faster with a strange fear that this letter meant I'd lose my new community. Inside I found a rectangle of heavy decorated paper. I pulled it out and watched the sunlight catch the holograms etched across its rectangular surface. The graphics filled the tiny space with as much artistic meaning and attention to detail as I thought humanly possible. The word "Evolution" sprawled across the top along with "Burning Man 2009." A picture resembled the elderly Charles Darwin with his brain exposed. A landscape of mystical creatures stretched far behind his portrait. On the back of the stub was the word "gift" in black glossy lettering. I rubbed my thumb on the word gift to make sure it wouldn't rub off. It stayed intact: my ticket to Burning Man!

A few of the crew had seen the exchange and started singing, *You got the golden ticket, you got the golden ticket!* Smiling like a cartoon character, I turned my face to hide my embarrassment. I wanted to hug every last one of these beautiful people I hardly knew. I started with Jess.

"Why are you guys giving me this ticket?" I questioned Jess, feeling my cheeks getting bright red. "Isn't there someone more deserving? I just showed up and you guys have been working for months."

Jess regarded me thoughtfully as she put her hand on my shoulder. "Rebecca and I have this philosophy that if someone feels like they own part of the piece, they account for its success. Look at the legs you cut out on Fishbug, Hassan! We wouldn't have had time to make them for this showing if you hadn't come in. You're our last minute angel."

I hesitated before responding still almost breathless. "Thanks so much for giving me a chance Jess." I took a look at the legs I had plasma cut welded to the frame of the legs. Up close all I could see were rough edges, but standing from a distance it fit in nicely with the rest of the art.

"Thanks for stepping through the door." She smiled. "What do you say? Do you want to come to Burning Man with us?"

Woozy from kindness intoxication, I got back to my task. I applied myself to my work twice as hard. Calling it work seemed like the wrong word. Work doesn't usually feel that good. And it wasn't charity, as I was getting back as much and even more than I was putting in. I'm not sure what it was, but it gave me tingles through my whole body. I'm going out on a limb and making up a word... philabouring. A mix of love, friendship, and labor perhaps? If you buy my word or not, I felt a deep gratitude towards these artists. They had been so kind to me, this random traveler, at a time when I needed it most. I was about to enter a dream within a dream. I was going to Burning Man with Fishbug!

Chapter 7

"A goal is not always meant to be reached, it often serves simply as something to aim at." — Bruce Lee

It was the last full workday before Fishbug's load-out to Burning Man. We did a full systems test, assembling the sculpture from top to bottom. Setting it up was the only real way to catch bugs we might encounter on the Playa.

For the first time I saw this elegant complex machine working with all its parts. The fire effects along the spine and tusks were aflame. The breathing thorax panels expanding and contracting in a slow graceful motion. The light show in the fiberglass brain was a window into the mind of Fishbug, projecting images of landscapes and the animals that lived there.

"Yay Fishbug!" Rebecca and Jess yelled.

"Yay Fishbug!" the rest of us answered at the top of our lungs, jumping up and down hugging each other with joy. Fishbug was ready to go! The Fishbug was beautiful.

As Rebecca and Jess began wrapping things up for the evening, I headed to my couch over-looking the shop floor for some much needed rest. I would need it. Tomorrow we needed to break her down, pack her up, and stick her on a flat bed headed for the Black Rock Desert in Nevada. It would surely be another late night for all of us.

On my way up the stairs, I smelled cigarette smoke wafting from the couch. On the top of the platform, I noticed it was Michelle triumphantly smoking her last of the evening. Everything about her was thick, from her arms to her Scottish accent. We'd been working together, but this was my first chance to chat with her.

"Hey there, I'm Michelle," she said. "I don't know if we've officially met yet. Rebecca told me all about you though. Welcome."

"Rebecca told me about you as well. She said to ask you about circumnavigating the globe on a sailboat. I assume you did that?"

"Oh that story huh?" She bellowed with laughter. I slid into an armchair next to her and got comfortable. "Ocean blue in a paint store makes me laugh now. Ain't nothing like the real thing. I had a friend tell me back in Scotland, *'Hey you're a single girl, you should buy a plane ticket to Fiji and crew a yacht.'* I finally got on a boat named *Freedom* heading to New Zealand from the UK. What a dodgy sailor that was. He was basically just winging it."

"Sounds intense." I tried to imagine a dodgy sailor holding my life in his hands.

"The boat had some serious issues. Broken mast. Leaky water tanks. It was a heap of shit and on top of that the crew had no experience."

"Holy shit! You still did it?"

"We'd stop every once in a while to bathe in the Atlantic. That was scary in itself, swimming in the middle of the ocean. I get chills down my neck just thinking about it. One day, I was swimming about and spotted something in the water. It was a glass bottle covered in barnacles and hermit crabs and a photo in it with an address on the back. The current of the Sargasso just carried it round and round for almost twenty years. I looked up the address on the note and showed up on her doorstep not two years later. A tiny old lady with huge character."

"Oh my god. Is she still living there?"

"I'm lucky to have gotten to meet her. Friend of mine to this day. Brilliant woman. I've met so many phenomenal people while traveling. You find so much generosity when you're open to it."

"I know how you feel." I was beginning to understand.

Michelle shifted in her seat and zipped up her bag. "I guess I should be letting you get to bed. We've got a big day tomorrow as you know! Rest well Hassan."

I stretched out on the beat up couch over looking the metal shop floor and pulled the dirty shop quilt over me. As I dreamed that night, ocean blue was everywhere. The possibilities endless.

I woke up a few hours later still in the dark of night. Everything was quiet. The whole shop was mine for a moment. *What an amazing journey,* I reflected. Michelle's story swallowed me whole with inspiration. That along with the amazing events of the past few weeks had brought me to the fork in the road. *Did I even want to go back to Boston?* Time was running out to make a decision as the subletter taking my room was due to move out at the end of August.

I slipped my shoes on and walked outside to see Fishbug. I set my hand onto the steel I had plasma cut my second day at the shop, now welded to the front legs. It was cold to my touch.

I loved my friends back home but I loved the idea of starting over too. I wouldn't mind a second chance. There was a lot to figure out, but maybe, always feeling like I needed a clear plan had been part of my problem in the first place. I knew it would be hard, lonely, and a ton of work, but I needed to listen to my heart, even if it had a hole in it. *Boston wasn't working for me.*

I thought about my job as a special ed teacher. The years of sticking with a teaching career because I was too scared to play music. Years of feeling like a fraud for not doing what I knew I needed to. *I'd had enough.* I thought about Maya, and how awful it felt to be reminded of her every time I slept in the bed we shared. It was torture. *I'd had enough.* I thought of how my mom, sister, and I had escaped to the East Coast all those long years ago. It was a place to hide, but I was done hiding. *I'd had enough! Boston wasn't working for me!*

I then thought about the music family I'd be leaving in Boston. It centered around the band I played guitar in. We practiced in the basement of my apartment on Dustin Street twice a week for two years. We played some amazing music but didn't really have a business plan. My last day in Boston before the road trip included me finishing up my overdubbed guitar tracks for our EP. That day almost seemed like a metaphor for a lot of things going wrong. There I was, trying to push someone else's project forward. Mark was an absolute phenom of a singer/songwriter, but at that time he wasn't motivated to be a full time performer. And no matter how hard I tried, that wasn't going to change unless Mark wanted it. Leaving the band in Boston was my note in a bottle. But I was done floating. *I'd had enough. Boston wasn't working for me.*

I looked at the yellow moon hanging over Fishbug. The light shimmered on the stainless steel tusks that would soon be on fire at Burning Man. It was a beautiful dust covered premonition. I thought of the passionate community that sculpted every precious piece of her. I thought of the leadership of Rebecca and Jess, who kept us motivated by being right beside us in the trenches every step of the way. Maybe the time had come to abandon a city and a community that wasn't serving me for a city and a community that was. *The only way to do that is to continue this amazing journey. I guess that's goodbye Boston. You were the most cantankerous friend I've ever had.*

Chapter 8

"Home is where one starts from." — TS Elliot

That next day may have been my longest day at the Shipyard yet. It took us all day, but by two in the morning we finally packed and loaded Fishbug onto the truck. Fitting each piece of the oddly shaped sculpture into the oddly shaped trailer may have been the most challenging game of Tetris I'd ever been a part of, but we finished the job and were still on speaking terms. The next morning, Fishbug would be headed to Burning Man.

A few days later, it became *my* turn to depart for Burning Man. Another Shipyard resident, Jay, agreed to rideshare out to Black Rock City with me. The two of us packed my car full of supplies and a single James Brown album I found stuffed behind a welder. We hit the road around midday.

Our route took us along I-80 East, and weaved through the heart of the Sierra Nevada mountain range. My Chevy's engine chugged along the steep inclines surrounded by forests of tall pines lining the road. In patches there were only steep sharp edges of rock that met the clear blue skyline. It occurred to me that if I continued down this interstate for another 3,000 miles it would take me all the way back within a mile of my apartment in Boston. I had other plans for this trip though.

After several hours, we finally made it to Reno, the last major city we'd pass before Burning Man. I drove by a giant sign at the entrance: 'The Biggest Little City in the World.' *Deja vu*, I thought to myself.

I pulled my car down the exit off the freeway and wove through the streets of downtown filled with the blinking lights of casinos. I turned into a gas station parking lot to pick up our water for the event. Jay and I walked inside and heard the ugly sounds of a wall full of slot machines against the far wall. *Ding. Ding. Ding. Ding. Woop. Woop. Woop. Woop.* We piled up gallon jug after gallon jug on the counter and the woman behind the checkout counter grinned at us with a mouth full of yellow stained teeth. "Headed to Burning Man?" she asked.

On the way out the door, I spotted an older gentleman by one of the slot machines. He looked to be around his late 50s. Nearly the same age as my dad. His blood shot eyes blankly stared into bright flashes of the slot machine in front of him, cigarette in one hand, cup of quarters in the other. The man sat alone looking vacant and depressed. Every crank of the slot machine handle emptied his pockets a little more. I imagined my dad gambling at the machine next to him.

*W*hen I was nine and my sister was seven, our dad took us on a trip to Reno. My parents had divorced the year before and my mom got full custody because the judge considered Dad a flight risk with us. Despite the flight risk status, Dad still got us over the summer for the next five years until Sara and I asked Mom to stop the visitations. A few weeks into our first summer on visitation he took us up I-80 through the Sierra and straight to Reno. His Lincoln Town Car careened the windy turns through the mountains. I peered out the car window as we glided past flimsy looking guardrails. My 9-year-old heart began to pound staring into the deep gorge and the snaked blue river crawling through it.

"Dad is this safe? How far down is that?"

"That's 7,000 feet. Don't worry, you're safe Hassan." He chuckled. I tightly gripped the handle of the car door in my right hand and my little sister's hand with my left hand.

A few hours later we got to the main strip in downtown Reno. From the freeway I saw casino after casino blinking in neon lights. We went under the beaming archway titled, 'Reno: The Biggest Little City in the World.' It looked to me like an amusement park. On the main strip we passed the Eldorado, Grande Sierra, and Gold Dust West. Finally we pulled into a parking lot in front of a tall building with Circus Circus written vertically on its side. Before we got out of the car, Dad sprayed two bursts of bitter cologne at his neck.

Dad held Sara in his arms as we walked over the cold marble cut floors of the lobby and onto the regal purple carpets in the game room. Thick wafts of cigarette smoke filled the heavy casino air as we skirted the main floor dinging and flashing with slot machines. He led us down to an arcade room with more blinking lights and handed both Sara and me a plastic cup full of quarters.

"I'll be back to get you both later," he told us before giving us both a cologne scented kiss and swaggering out onto the casino floor.

In that moment I saw a man who saw the world through one eye. The other was made of glass. Mom to this day isn't sure what happened. My uncles told me his eye was knocked out by a shoe thrown at him by my grandfather in a fit of rage. The glass eye that made him ashamed of his appearance. The glass eye that made him escape Jordan at the age of 16 to be homeless on the snowy streets of Germany while he awaited medical treatment. The glass eye that led him to abuse our mom as he had been abused. The eye that made him numb the pain with booze and gambling. The eye that brought us to the lonely arcade room in Circus Circus.

Sara wandered away from my sight and I went straight for Sonic Wings. I dropped in my first quarter and began shooting down enemy planes for hours. Sara was done with her bucket of quarters first and sat next to me by the arcade machine. On my last quarter I ended up beating the game. "Sara, I beat the game," I said gleefully. She rolled her seven-year-old eyes. I proudly put my name into the high score box. I had never beaten an arcade game before, or since.

It occurred to Sara first. "Where's Dad? I'm hungry."

"I don't know."

Another hour passed as my sister and I watched the gamers come in and out of the room from our spot at the front of the arcade. We were trapped in a neon blinking nightmare.

"Where's Dad?" Sara asked me again as we sat on the popcorn and trash littered carpet of the game room. We both began to cry.

The manager of the arcade rushed over. She crouched down to our level and spoke to us softly. "What's wrong? Where's your parents?" We sobbed harder.

"We don't know. Can you find our dad?" I said in-between tears.

"I don't know where he is either. But we'll look for him," she consoled us.

I don't remember if she found him or if he eventually came back on his own, whether he got in trouble and blamed us, what time it was when we got home or how we spent the rest of the vacation. What I do remember is not wanting to visit him after that. And everytime I hear the sound of slot machines I feel some happiness sucked out of me.

"Are you in a hurry?" Jay asked as we got on the highway running past Reno. The entire back seat of my car sloshed from the stacked gallons of water obstructing my rear visibility.

"No. Sorry." I slowed my car down a bit to just five miles over the limit.

"No worries. Is this your first year?" Jay asked as she retied her white bandanna holding back her dirty blonde hair.

"It is."

"I am a first year too," she responded. "I've been on the West Coast for a while and I've heard peoples opinions on both sides. A lot criticize Burning Man. There is a bandwagon associated with it, or even sometimes that the festival is just unsustainable.

"It's all new for me. I'm a blank slate." The dry landscape rushed by as I switched out of the slow lane.

"The ironic thing is that the people with the harshest opinions usually have never been. I don't think people should talk shit or talk it up. People should do their own cost-benefit analysis when they get there."

We got off the I-80 exit and headed north up Route 437. The road narrowed and for the most part, was deserted. Further up, we drove through the Pyramid Lake reservation. The town looked very poor. Old broken-down trucks and trailers littered the landscape. Spray-painted signs for Indian tacos dotted the highway.

We drove further out of town and watched the sun fall behind the mountains cradling Pyramid Lake. About an hour longer on the road, and we passed through another small town called Gerlach. It had one gas station, one restaurant, and a few hundred people. The traffic grew thicker as we continued our pilgrimage.

It was pitch dark by the time we finally arrived at the festival. There were no lights on the road and the entrance was difficult to find. Luckily, Jay saw the orange Special Event sign. I swung my car down the unpaved road, keeping my foot light on the gas, my eyes growing steadily wider in anticipation. Dust kicked up into the night sky as we made our way down the thoroughfare. The lights glowing in the distance from the festival served as a beacon. We were almost there.

We got to the gate and handed our tickets to a guy with bright yellow goggles and a dusty leather vest that had pieces of fabric hanging from the bottom trim. His partner requested we get out of the vehicle while they searched it.

"Do you guys have any drugs?"

"No," I responded.

"That's a shame." He shook his head laughing. Jay and I chuckled too.

A half-mile up the dimly lit road we were stopped again at the entrance to the festival grounds. We were at the threshold of another world.

"Welcome home!" the men outside yelled. They pulled us out of the car and gave us big hugs, covering our clean clothes with a layer of playa dust.

"Are you two virgins?" they asked, implying this was our first time at Burning Man.

"Yes," we answered. The two men's eyes glowed. The man handed me a hammer and gestured to an oversized bell in front of us.

"Ring the bell to let the citizens of Black Rock City know of your arrival." I gripped the handle and gave the bell a smack. My ears rang as the metal vibrated. Jay then grabbed the hammer and smacked it three or four more times.

The dusty man nodded approvingly. "Put your hands in the dirt." I looked over at Jay to make sure I wasn't the only one doing it. "Now take two fistfuls of playa dust and rub it all over yourselves." I grabbed two handfuls and began spreading the dust on my clothes and skin.

"Alright," the man said. "Now spank each other."

"You first," Jay said. I cautiously bent over and she slapped my ass with the open palm of her hand. She bent over and I whacked her next. We both started laughing uncontrollably.

"Welcome home!" they called. I started my engine and shifted into drive looking into the dark road ahead swirling with dust and sand. We were at the border of another world and there was no going back. A *leap of faith.*

Lights glimmered brighter and brighter in the distance as we got closer. Hundreds of signs placed about ten feet apart lined the road. On each one was part of a quotation. Jay read them aloud as we drove by.

"If creation is," she announced. A few feet later, "An alternative." We slowed. "To evolution. Then we should. Also teach. Stork theory. As an alternative. To sexual. Reproduction. It is not. The strongest. Of the species. Or the intelligent. But it is the one. That is the most. Adaptable. To change. In the long history. Of human kind. And animals too. Those who learned to collaborate." She frowned. "Missed one. Most effectively. Have prevailed. By Charles Darwin." I slowed the car to make it easier for her to read.

"You're a monkey. You are a. Slightly clever. Pants wearing. Primate. If you forget. You're a monkey. Fashioned on the. Plains. Being chased by. Tigers. You shouldn't invest. Aware of your. Own psychology. That is why we. As investors. Get panicked. Its why we. Sell out. At the bottom. What but. The wolf's tooth. Whittled so fine. The fleet of limbs. Of the antelope. What but fear. Winged the birds. And hunger. Jeweled. With such eye's. The Great. Goshawk's head. By Robinson Jeffers."

The signs continued. "Since when has. The world of. Computer software. Design. Been about. What people want. This is a simple. Question of. Evolution. The day is. Quickly coming. When every knee. Will bow down. To a silicon fist. And you will all. Beg your. Binary gods. For mercy. By Bill Gates." Intense, I thought as Jay finished. The signs stretched on and on as we drove, tricking us into driving the 10mph speed limit the entire way.

I stopped the car as we entered the rim opening to the art sculptures in the center of Burning Man. Jay and I got out to observe. Stars shone overhead as we peered across the lit up horizon. In the distance, at the center of our view, was the unmistakably Man of Burning Man. He stood straight up and glowed bright yellow, dwarfing all the other art sculptures around him. Work lights shone at many of the projects erected along the horizon. People were busy getting ready for the opening.

One of the big electric work lights belonged to Fishbug. I could make out the dangerous looking fire breathing monster all the way across the Playa. Almost instinctually, Jay and I left my vehicle and ran as fast as we could to the work site. That's the only place we wanted to be.

"Woohoo!" the crew yelled when we got there. They gave each of us warm dusty hug.

Rebecca approached me. "Hassan, I already got a compliment on the Fishbug legs you plasma cut! I wanted to tell you. Congrats!"

I glanced over to look at the legs. *I did that.* The legs looked to be pulling Fishbug out of the ground. It didn't look easy. *Was she*

struggling too? I took in the whole picture of Fishbug, from the fishtail to the tusks projecting off her face. Fishbug had never looked so good to me. She looked absolutely beautiful. Burning Man was a good home for her.

I walked over to the tail for a closer look and saw a pair of legs and black Converse high tops sticking out the open hatch at the tail.

"Hey, I'm Tad. You're Hassan, right?" a voice called from inside the tail. "I think we met back at the shop. Can you hold this flashlight on these wires?" He indicated the red Maglight by pointing his foot. I grabbed the light from the hook in the tail door and shined it inside. It illuminated a complexity of wires and hoses woven together in a way that looked like actual organic anatomy.

"What did you just do?" I asked, in awe of the electronic wizardry he made look so easy.

"Oh, I just fixed the linear actuator."

"Linear actuator..." I repeated sounding a little perplexed.

"It's what controls the three mechanical functions of Fishbug; the fire, breathing, and lights. The fire along the spine goes from taller to shorter every 40 seconds which is synchronized at the same rate that the side panels expand and contract, giving it the aesthetic of organic breathing. The egg lights inside the thorax are also synced up to this system as well."

"It all happens at the same time?"

"The linear actuator supports the aesthetic goal of making Fishbug come to life as one synchronized organism. It's actually pretty simple. Lever valves are mounted along the length of the linear actuator, which goes back and forth with the power of a small motor and an Arduino micro processor. The valves are opened and closed creating the effects you see as a spectator."

"Arduino," I muttered.

Tad sat up out of the tail and wiped his hands. "The fuel valve is pushed by a lever and adds more propane to the system, which creates the high flame effect. When the air valve is pushed, it sends air into the system and inflates the suspension bags in the spine, causing the side panels to expand. The lever moves back and forth on a timer, synchronizing the whole system."

"Wow," I said quietly.

I set the light back inside the tail when Tad finished his work. I left to ask Jess and Rebecca if they needed help as well, but they insisted that Jay and I allow our bodies to get acclimated to the harsh desert environment. "Drink lots of water and take it easy for at least 24 hours," they instructed. "Eating salty food also helps your body retain liquids, so try that too."

I took the free time as an opportunity to explore. I jumped on my bike and careened the Playa, weaving through the glowing monuments scattered across the landscape. I had more questions than answers of the beautiful outdoor art menagerie. In the distance I saw a subtle glow of orange, not flashy like the other sculptures.

I pedaled hard, bouncing on rough patches of sand. What I had seen as a mere orange speck across the Playa was up close an enormous temple shaped like a lotus flower and three stories high. The subtle beauty was a quiet invitation.

I dropped my bike by the yellow caution tape that lined the temple's perimeter. The crew was working late putting on the finishing touches. In my research I had learned that this temple was the spiritual epicenter of Burning Man. On the walls people left shrines to loved ones lost, poems, memories, and watched them all engulfed in cathartic flames on the last day of Burning Man. *What should I write on the temple?* I wondered. *What would I let go?* I half wanted to sneak under the caution tape and explore this intriguing piece. *Another day,* I thought as I rode off.

Chapter 9

"My great concern is not whether you failed, but whether you are content with your failure." — Abraham Lincoln

The next morning, I woke with a fine layer of dust on everything inside my tent, including myself. All around were the sounds of the clinking hammers on tent stakes. The city was growing right before my ears.

Looking at my tent from the outside made it obvious to me that my living situation still needed work. The rebar holding my shade structure's ropes teetered at the slightest touch and severely needed to be driven further into the ground. The frying pan I had used in place of the hammer I forgot to buy was protruding from the sand covered in rough rebar marks.

I made my way out to Fishbug to find the crew already hard at work. When I went to put my hand on the doorknob of the shed to get my gloves a violent gust of wind and sand blew it open, taking me along with it.

"Dust storm!" yelled Poe, Fishbug's computer science expert.

My eyes began to sting from the pelting sand. With my free hand I slipped on my goggles. Fishbug, the crew, and the whole work site had literally disappeared in the whiteout. I could hear them though, as they made sounds like they were riding a bull at a rodeo.

When the storm passed we continued on as if nothing had happened. "Hey, can someone give me a hand with these bins?" I looked over and saw Judy under the shade structure. Judy had smooth dark skin and straight jet-black hair hanging about shoulder length.

"I'll help," I offered, getting a glimpse of the see-though plastic bins filled with white fabric stacked up near the propane tanks. The two of us lugged bin after bin into the stomach of Fishbug and set them along the back wall.

She climbed up a blue ladder with a cluster of sheets in her hands. As my neck craned to view her work I was reminded of the image of Michelangelo painting the Sistine chapel on his back. While she manipulated one length of fabric I heard a loud static pop. "Ouch!" she said dropping what she was holding.

"You okay? Can I help?" I asked gathering the cloth to hand back to her.

"I'm fine. Pulling the fabric charged up my hands. There's nothing I can do really. The tips of my fingers have been tingling from all the shocks though. It would take forever to get someone up to speed with an understanding both of the lengths and tensions needed for every single piece of fabric. If we were back at the Shipyard that'd be another story, but this all has to be done by tomorrow."

From the other side of the site Jess's voice called for a meeting. We circled up as Jess went over the plan of attack.

"Ok everyone. Great job so far. We've been invited to Camp Tree Ring Circus at 7:30 and Esplanade this evening. Everyone take an artist medallion to get fed! Let's meet around dusk."

I looked at the shiny medal as she dropped it into my hand. It felt smooth to the touch. The black letters popped out: *Feed the artists; burn the art.* That might as well have been an Olympic gold medal in my dusty hand. It said I was an artist. It felt good hearing, but I had a ways to go on my journey to prove it though. *I still needed to write music.*

When my work was done, I took off on my bike for a tour of the Playa and art installations. I passed an enormous metal

structure in the shape of two gigantic communicating neurons.
Metal branches projected from the two cores that represented
neurons, connected by a stainless steel arch.

Biking further, I saw a silver object in the thick clouds of
dust. The wind settled, revealing a 60-foot stainless steel rocket. I
half expected to see Marvin the Martian step out of the cockpit.

I began to pedal away from the Rocket only to be hit by a
huge gust of wind that nearly knocked me off my bike. It gave me
a sudden realization. My tent was still unsecured. It had been all
day. "Oh fuck!" I muttered.

I raced back along the Esplanade, weaving through art cars,
costumed cyclists, and naked pedestrians to my campsite on Chaos
Street as fast as my feet could pedal. The wind picked up and
another cloud of dust hit me nearly sending me flying off my seat.
Everything white. Dirt and sand attacked my body as I pedaled,
making its way into my mouth and lungs. I did my best not to take
full breaths as I slogged through the angry desert.

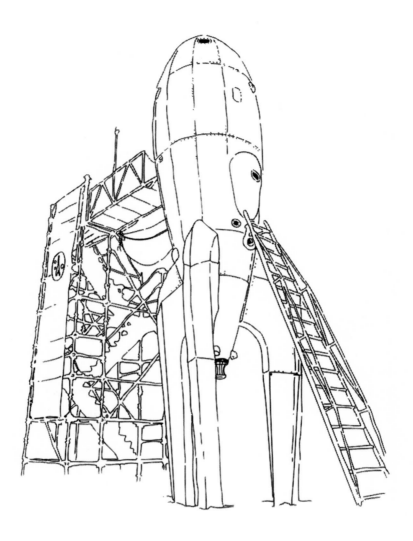

I made it back to camp to find Jay's tent was blowing away.
I dropped my bike in the sand and grabbed her rain tarp in mid-
air before it sailed away. I shoved some rebar stakes into the ground
as best I could by hand. Then another stake came out, and another
piece of the tent flew off.

I secured what I could but realized I needed help. The winds were too strong. But, when I hopped on my bike, as soon as my right foot made a full arc, my back tire and chain completely dislodged slamming me to the desert floor. Blood dripped from my wounded limbs. From the ground I observed that my tent was now blowing away too. "Bastard tent!" I yelled into the white dust cloud. Hobbling over to the shade structure, I held onto one end of the roof as the legs wobbled back and forth. More of Jay's tent was blowing away behind me as I held on. "Oh Fuck it all!"

As if on cue, Jay showed up. She diffused my temper with some calm words and we began to put our camp back together. We secured her tent first and put in five new two-foot rebar stakes at the weak points. I pulled my car behind the shade structure and used that as another anchor point. For peace of mind, I tied everything to everything again – it wasn't going anywhere now. While I was working, Jay managed to put my bike back together.

I sat in my camp chair with my first aid kit to clean my wounds. As I swabbed the cuts, my blood dripped onto the ground. The desert sand drank the drops like quicksand. I winced in pain. *Would that be enough for the angry playa gods?* I wondered. *What other trials did they have in store?* All the research hadn't fully prepared me for the awesome power of nature at Burning Man. The desert awed and terrified me at the same time. It was one of the harshest and most indifferent climates I'd ever been in. I think everyone at Burning Man that day felt the warning. The desert was to be feared and respected.

As I cleaned my cut I thought of two of the principles of Burning Man: radical self-reliance and communal effort. I began to understand. Until you are actually on the desert, far from stores filled with food, water, and supplies, you don't fully realize how vulnerable you'll be. We had to be smart. We were exposed. We needed each other to survive.

Chapter 10

"He is not a lover who does not love forever." — Euripides

When I arrived at Tree Ring Circus for the artist dinner most of the Fishbug crew was already there. A hearty aroma pulled me toward the kitchen table.

"Get it while it's hot!" Wendy shouted, holding a big steaming pot with two large oven mitts.

"LET'S HEAR IT FOR WENDY!" a voice shouted.

"THANK YOU WENDY!" we answered in unison at the top of our lungs. Wendy smiled shyly and did a quick curtsey, only to head back to work organizing her kitchen crew. One by one we got fed, a healthy portion of fresh green pea soup mixed with diced carrots, onions, leeks, and fat red lima beans.

As people milled about after dinner, I made eye contact with an attractive blonde woman at the party. She gave me an inviting smile.

"What's your name?" I asked as I approached her.

"My name's Goldilox. This is my first year at Burning Man."

"That's not your real name, is it?"

"It's my Playa name. Someone from my camp gave it to me." She tugged a braid of her bright blonde hair.

"Playa name huh? I see. I think I'm going to stick with Hassan," I joked. "You know, you remind me of an old friend of mine. She was a great teacher."

"I'm a teacher too." She beamed.

We kept chatting and found ourselves wandering further

and further away from the rest of the gathering, until the voices there were only a low murmur in the background. We grabbed a seat on an open patch of Playa. My heart beat a little harder.

After more conversation, she snaked her arm around mine and took my hand, caressing my palm with her fingertips. The weight of her body leaned into my shoulder. It was good to hold her.

"You feel great," I said as I fell deeper into the moment with her.

Her sleepy eyes stared back at me. "You too." Her voice was as smooth as silk.

We soon found ourselves kissing against a backdrop of starlight. My lips felt electric against hers. She slipped her bra off and lay on top of me in the sand, her soft breasts pressed up against my body.

When she finally said goodbye she told me to come by her campsite and visit her. I watched her walk away gracefully as the cool night air swept in around me. She turned and waved before disappearing into the darkness.

I sat alone under the Playa moon and put my hand in the sand where Goldilock laid moments before, my heart still pounding.

I felt a cool breeze sweep through and I shivered. Being close to Goldilox made me ache for a meaningful connection. Maybe deep down all I really wanted was love. Love to plug the hole in my heart.

Maya came to my mind. She always did when I got close to someone. The way she felt, smelled, tasted. How her voice used to sound when we lay next to each other. "Get out of my head woman!" I shouted internally.

In the distance I saw the Temple. Something called me to it. Maybe I'd find the answers I was looking for. I got on my bike and pointed my handlebars directly at the softly glowing structure in the distance. A cold wind whipped at my face as I pedaled faster and faster, my heart pounding and sweat beads dripping from my forehead. I rushed to get there as if it were a mirage that was about to disappear.

When I got close, I noticed the caution tape had been taken down. I climbed the staircase to the top floor of the temple and looked out over the Playa.

On a railing next to the staircase I noticed a small shrine had been set up. Rocks and candles surrounded a picture of a woman. A sealed letter was placed underneath one of the larger stones. On it it said, *I'll always miss you. I'll look for you in heaven.*

A black Sharpie sat on the floor by my feet. I wanted to write something of my own, but what? No one I knew had died. The person who left the picture probably knew real pain. My head began to ache and I massaged my forehead. I knew I didn't really miss Maya. Not like this. She was making me miserable, but that's not the same as missing someone.

A person I did miss popped into my head though. Someone I didn't think about too often. A woman I should have actually been upset about losing.

I met Sarah in Chicago on my first cross-country road trip in the summer of 2006. We were in the same checkout line at Whole Foods. With knots in my stomach, I gave her my number asking for a tour of Chicago while I was in town. I drove away never expecting to hear from her again. Love was always a tricky thing for me. I believed I wasn't worthy of it. It was really hard for me to not get into my head about having a cleft lip. Getting close to someone meant I'd have to confront this part of myself that I felt so ashamed about. It opened a time capsule of suffering.

*W*hen a child is born with a cleft lip their soft and hard pallet don't grow together correctly, leaving a hole in their mouth, exposing the sinus cavity and an opening in their lip. It's a condition that makes for a surgery filled childhood. I went under the knife related to my cleft pallet just shy of ten times before I was ten.

When the doctor handed me to my mother in the delivery room she was shocked at first. She remembers blaming herself. The doctor tried his best to reassure her it wasn't her fault. Though she didn't know why at the time, Mom later remarked that the doctors and nurses kept a close eye on her. She later learned that there is a high risk of mothers abandoning babies born with this condition. She and Dad loved me all the same though, despite my complicated medical problems. While I was still screaming in my mother's arms, Dad immediately ran to the wing of the Kaiser hospital to find one of the best cleft pallet doctors in Northern California. Dr. Koo went on to be the surgeon for all my early corrective operations.

While I obviously have no memory of my life as an infant, I imagine life was very painful for baby me. At three months, I had corrective surgery on my soft and hard pallet leaving me with 300 stiches. Mom was forced to feed me through a rubber syringe with small holes at the end because of how sensitive my mouth was. Mom says when she got home with me after the surgery the entire house was clean. It was the only time she recalls Dad cleaning the place in their seven-year marriage. Getting to sleep was always difficult for me as I'd toss and turn, wailing for hours. Mom tells me she cried a lot too. Sometimes the only thing that would soothe me was a slow drive around the neighborhood in her baby blue Volkswagen Rabbit.

To celebrate the milestone of me turning one-year-old, Mom and Dad brought me to get my picture taken at Sears. The woman working the camera was uncomfortable and squirmed at the sight of me. "Do you want me to turn his face?"

"Why would we want to do that?" Mom retorted. By the time I had turned one, Mom and Dad were used to the weird looks people would give me. Both her and Dad still have their copy of the 8 X10 picture of me smiling wide on their living room mantles 3,000 miles apart from one another.

At 18 months I had another surgery to repair my unformed lip. Again, I cried and cried and had lots of trouble sleeping. After the operation, they sent me home with a pair of "no no" arm braces I had to put on so I wouldn't touch my healing mouth. For a few months post surgery I'd have to wear them almost all day, unable to bend my elbows. I had many sets, all different sizes for the different surgeries growing up.

A few times a day Mom would rub coco butter on my lip to minimize the scarring. Mom would also dab hydrogen peroxide on my mouth with a cue tip in an effort to keep everything clean. I still managed to get colds and infections all the time. In particular, I had a lot of ear infections. The doctors used to put tubes in my ears to drain the fluid. My ear canal is still scarred from those years.

At around two, I started speech therapy. A woman would come over and record my speaking. She'd play games with me getting me to make all sorts of sounds and blow a ball of paper with a straw across the kitchen table. If I said a word wrong she'd correct me. Mom say that I learned how to say words so correctly, I would correct my younger sister Sara if she didn't enunciate.

At around ten I started getting orthodontic care from a doctor in Plymouth named Dr. Cressman. Mom points to moments like this as signs of serendipity as Dr. Cressman was one of the few orthopedic doctors who had experience working with cleft pallets in our corner of Massachusetts. His office was also only a half mile away from my grandparents' house in Plymouth.

The first year I saw Dr. Cressman I was fitted with a pallet expander. My mouth was too small and needed a crank each week to get me ready for braces. Each one would dig into my gums and spread my mouth apart incrementally.

At age eleven Dr. Cressman fitted me with braces, which I kept on until the end of high school. My braces allowed each tooth to glacially move around in my gums into their correct position. At thirteen, Dr. Cressman also recommended that I get a bone graft to build up the bone in my mouth. The goal was to eventually attach an implant to fill the gaping hole in the upper left quadrant of my gums. Mom used her insurance from working at M & M Sporting Goods to cover my surgery at New England Medical Center.

The day of the surgery the doctors had me count back from ten as the anesthetics filled my blood stream and everything went black. While I was under, the surgeons cut me near my hip and cut out two small chunks of bone, fitting the bone into my gums. I woke up from the surgery dazed and swollen. It took me a few days to get out of bed and a few weeks to walk without pain. I still have nerve damage from the surgery on both hips. On the way home from surgery Mom had a country music radio station on. Billy Ray Cyrus's twangy voice came through our speakers singing "Achy Breaky Heart." We cranked up the volume and sang along at the top of our lungs.

I remember being a pretty positive kid overall but in dark moments I'd break down and express my frustration with everything to Mom. Sometimes she'd catch me punching myself in the face, totally disgusted with who I was. I later learned Mom gave me the same advice she was getting from Gram about what ailed her. "We aren't born with problems that are too much for us. It's how you deal with them that makes the difference."

I'd need to remember Mom's words while in high school. Having an obvious physical deformity during my years at Plymouth North High School was social death. I was subhuman. Or at least I felt that way. I could go on at length about the many incidents I experienced bullying by both kids and adults, but one class and one kid epitomizes what life was like growing up in Plymouth with a cleft pallet.

It was in my sophomore Social Studies class. Normally Social Studies had been my favorite subject. I loved the stories and being transported back in time. Unfortunately, a kid named Chris sat in front of me my entire sophomore year in Ms. Laraquente's class. I could barely see the chalkboard around the guy he was so huge. Every day he'd turn around and say something like, "Did your face get kicked by a camel?" Though the insults would evolve, they usually involved putting me down for being Arab and having a cleft lip. The experience was like being repeatedly branded everyday with a hot iron. The other kids would snicker as I sat there, afraid to speak up. My teacher would sit idly by and let it happen usually without saying a word. I went from being a straight A student from elementary to middle school to a C student in high school.

I had one final operation my sophomore year of college. My last procedure's goal was to put in a tooth implant. I woke up from the operating room swollen and sore. For two weeks it looked like I had been punched in the mouth.

About six months later I went back to New England Medical Center and they put the tooth on the post. I truly wish they had put me under for this as it was the most painful thing that has happened to me as an adult. I sat in the doctor's recliner fully lucid as they stuck needles and other metal objects in my gums. I remember gripping the arms of my chair white knuckled with tears coming out of my eyes; each moment feeling like a mini eternity.

I look back on my history of surgeries with complex emotions. I'll probably be sorting this out my whole life in some way. The worst part about it all was that I felt completely alone. There was nothing anyone could do or say to make it better. It was my burden to carry.

*T*o my surprise, Sarah called me the next day after our chance encounter at Whole Foods. We agreed to meet at a bar in downtown Chicago. My eyes widened as she approached my table. Sarah had big beautiful hazel eyes and pouting rosy lips to match her burgundy hair. She might have been the most beautiful woman I had ever seen. So pretty, I convinced myself that she was doing me an obligatory Midwestern courtesy by meeting me. I did my best to hide the butterflies. *What do I have to lose?* I told myself to relax.

During lunch I was nervous at first, watching everything closely. I asked her what she did and found out that she was also a teacher, about to get her Masters in School Administration with the hopes of one day becoming a principal of an elementary school. Sarah was as passionate as they come. She'd often stay late to help her ELS students get up to speed. We started trading stories back and forth and had each other laughing our heads off. I'm not sure at what point but somewhere in-between teacher stories I let my guard down.

After lunch, we left the bar to a crack of thunder and a downpour. We bolted to my car for shelter.

"You still in the mood to give me a tour?" I asked before getting in.

"Of course." She smiled back from under her umbrella.

We navigated through the heavy rain to the sound of Sarah singing along to a Ray Charles album.

Night and Day. Night and Day…. Squeeze me tight and Make everything alright. I know the Night time is the Right time, to be with the one you love.

After 20 minutes or so we pulled over at what seemed to be the height of the storm. Oddly enough, as soon as we stopped, the rain stopped too. In an instant the sun was out.

We had landed next to a conservatory of flowers in the heart of Chicago. We entered the clear glass building to witness their flower garden in full bloom. Roses, orchids, and magnolias bursting color and sweet smells.

"I think we are the only ones here," Sarah observed. She placed her hand in mine. The whole conservatory was our private Garden of Eden. Her eyes invited me to kiss her and I did. We didn't stop kissing for the whole week I was in Chicago. We couldn't stop. We didn't want to.

The last time we saw each other was in the back of a yellow cab the day before I left. She had to speak at a big fundraiser she was organizing for breast cancer. She gave me a long kiss. I slipped my hand under her skirt and realized she wasn't wearing underwear. I inched my hand along her soft thigh and then inside her. We both gasped and in a flash of light, had a simultaneous orgasm, leaving the two of us twitching and wanting more in the backseat of the taxi.

"Put away that wallet!" she ordered as I attempted to pay the fare.

I didn't hear from her until the next morning on the highway to Denver. She explained why she hadn't called. The fundraiser she helped host that night lasted much longer than she expected and raised much more than expected, to the tune of $100,000. I almost turned back. Maybe I should have.

Sarah was on my mind the whole rest of my road trip. One day I checked my email inbox and she had sent me this Irish Blessing:

May the road rise to meet you,
May the wind be always at your back.
May the sun shine warm upon your face,
The rains fall soft upon your fields.
And until we meet again,
May God hold you in the palm of his hand.

I had never felt that warm before in my whole life. When I got back to Boston, we spoke over the phone almost every day for about six more months. We were falling in love from a distance. We even started talking about the possibility of me moving to Chicago to be with her. I was looking at jobs and apartments and she was an extra set of eyes on my resumes.

When it came time to commit to that decision though, I chickened out. My rationale was that she was about to be a principal of a school and I was a struggling artist who didn't even make art. I thought she'd stop loving me if she got to know the real me.

I'd missed Sarah for years at that point. She was stuck in my heart like an unopened time capsule. I was only 23 at the time we met and thought that it'd be easy to have an experience like that again. Years were slipping by though and I really hadn't met anyone I felt such a deep connection to. Maya was the only woman I had opened up to in all that time.

I set my hands onto the railing of the temple and peered far off into the distance. The sky was near pitch black. *Maybe I was trying to force the relationship I never got to have with Sarah onto Maya? I never thought of it like that. Do you get more than one shot to be with a woman like Sarah? Did I miss my chance?* I felt a few hot tears stream down my face.

I left the black Sharpie on the floor of the Temple. I wasn't quite ready to write anything. There were still too many questions I had to answer.

Chapter 11

"As we look ahead into the next century, leaders will be those who empower others." — Bill Gates

I woke up the next morning and measured the sun to be about four fingers pointed sideways over the mountains. Time was a fluid thing at Burning Man in part because no one had a clock readily available. All we had on the Playa most of the time was the distant Sun over the horizon. The Fishbug crew often used what they coined as the "finger method" to schedule group meetings. I adopted it too.

The city had grown considerably overnight. There was almost no space left around my campsite. An RV had pulled up beside my spot and a car with a trailer had pulled up behind me. They called themselves Camp Spontaneous Salad and were comprised of three people from Ojai, California.

I walked over to Rebecca's tent on the edge of Biology Street where a few people were drinking coffee and slurping down freshly cooked Asian noodles. They offered me both. While I slurped, I observed how much more prepared they were than I. Deep inside a carport, their tent was safe from the elements, carefully staked with an *actual* sledgehammer. They had a table with kitchen gear and coolers full of tasty-looking food. They also had a lot of useful items like bungee cords, zip ties, extra propane, a handle of Jim Beam, and a can opener. My coolers were full of food that one might find in a prison cafeteria.

At about midday, I made my way to Fishbug. There was still much to do, and the official opening of the festival was only a day away. We needed to have another fire safety meeting, get the projectors working, hook up our plumbing, weave the fabric on the inside of the bug, and do a full test run of all the working parts together. There was no time to waste.

I got right to work when I arrived, helping a team digging a three-foot trench for our propane lines, extension cords, and air hoses. Sweat dripped off our faces as the sun beat down on our backs. Every gust was a welcome relief from the dry heat.

"You're a new face here. I don't think we met at the Shipyard. I'm Gary." Gary dripped in sweat next to me with a shovel of his own. He stopped to retie the bandana over his long strands of playafied hair. Though we had never officially met, I had seen Gary around the work sight often, usually working directly with the heavy machinery team at Burning Man to move large parts of Fishbug.

"How did you get involved here?" I asked.

"That's a long story."

"We got time," I said looking at the long distance we still had to dig.

"I was working as a foreman on rigging crews. It was pretty stressful, overseeing huge cranes and having so many lives depend on you. Three years ago, a guy I was working with fell from four-hundred feet." Gary paused a moment to rub his forehead. "I saw him hit a beam on the way down. He died right there. I put my notice in that day."

"I'm sorry. That's awful."

"It got me here. Working on this gorgeous beast." Gary rubbed Fishbug's tail. "They're putting my skills to good use. Bringing art to the people. It feels good."

"I know how you feel."

"At the Fire Arts Festival a few months back, I saw Fishbug

set up for the first time. I thought, what is this thing? It was just a white funky looking metal frame. But when the side panels came on and the brain got attached, it all started to come together. And then there was the fire." Gary's eyes lit up. "I can't really explain the satisfaction. We had taken a couple of steel poles and turned it into this bad-ass sculpture."

"How long have you been working with Jess and Rebecca?"

"It's been a good four or five months now. And the ladies are awesome." Gary grinned. "It's a different energy, for sure. It's not like working for guys. There are never any put-downs. I never want to tell them to fuck off. They're actual leaders, but they give other people leadership too. I know quite a bit about running crews, but those two have taught me a lot."

"ROUND UP!" I heard Jess's voice shout out.

The team packed under the shade structure and formed a circle around her. "Ok everyone. Great work. We are almost ready for primetime. We are going to do a walk through of each step of lighting Fishbug. Everyone who thinks they will sign up for fire safety shifts find Michelle." Michelle raised her hand. "She will show where to lay out wet towels and extinguishers. We will also need a few people to be assigned to starting up the generator and air compressor. If you're interested find Gary."

"I'll be near the cooler," Gary belted. We all howled with laughter.

Jess continued. "People who want to learn about how to turn on the propane tanks and get the ball valve fittings open head to the fuel depot with Rebecca. Those that want to do the lighting follow Mathew. Let's light her up!"

We all broke into our teams and got brief instructions before starting. I joined with the fire safety crew.

"Gary, start the compressor!" Jess shouted.

Fishbug lit up without a hitch. Each of us got a turn to shoot the flame cannons to our absolute delight. I was entranced watching every one of the sixteen fire effects along the spine oscillate as the side panels expanded and contracted. Fishbug was alive and it was gorgeous.

"YEAH FISHBUG!" Jess shouted.

"FISHBUG! WOHOOOOOO!" We all screamed at the top of our lungs.

Once we had wrapped up the week's scheduling, Jess informed us that we were invited to another artist's dinner at a different camp later that evening. Our medallions from the night before would still be valid. We went our separate ways into the dust possibly all wondering the same thing. *What's for dinner?*

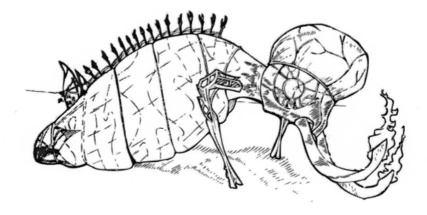

Chapter 12

.

"Every artist was first an amateur." — Ralph Waldo Emerson

"Hey, get up. We're late for the free meal!" Jay tugged at my tent. I quickly hopped outside struggling with a shirt button while slipping on my shoes. Jay and I did a light jog over to Camp Seed for supper, hoping the food wasn't all gone.

We arrived out of breath. At first glance though, it seemed we had rushed for no reason. The crew was nowhere to be found. Under the canopy, I saw a six year old boy with spiky blonde hair trot from the back of the kitchen. He came up next to where we sat clad in a zebra striped t-shirt and black gloves with the fingers cut out. He thrust out a hand for a shake and introduced himself. "Welcome to Camp Seed. My name is Brian, but you can call me Screaming Falcon."

The boy's father left a boiling pot of water on the stove and came over to where the three of us sat. "I thought you were Fire Ninja!" he said to his son.

"No, I'm Screaming Falcon now."

"Is this your first year?" I asked the boy.

"No, this is my fourth year," Screaming Falcon replied.

"Wow! Impressive. What's your favorite thing about Burning Man?"

"The dust storms and not having to bathe everyday," Screaming Falcon answered candidly.

"Mine too!" We both had a laugh.

Time passed and people began to appear, but no one from our crew. It turned out there had been a miscommunication and Jay and I were at the wrong dinner. Our crew was over at Poe's camp having noodles. We were at the Flaming Lotus Girls artist dinner for the crew who built Soma.

"Dinner's served!" Screaming Falcon called as they began bringing steaming vegetarian pasta.

"Hey there. What's your name?" A woman with short brown hair covered in a dusty cowboy hat asked me.

"My name's Hassan. I'm with Fishbug."

"Oh, I heard about you from Rebecca. My name's Catie. I think it's brave of you jumping onto the Fishbug crew like you have." I felt my cheeks get red. "I dropped in green like you too."

"Thanks for that. I'm learning so much from them."

"Stick around and you'll learn more. I remember the first time I showed up at FLG. I was on the outside of their meeting circle. I felt like I didn't fit in. All these people know what they're doing and I had no experience. I was just about to leave, but I caught myself and said 'Hey Catie, take a step into the circle. It's going to be okay.' They taught me how to be a metal worker. I even built one of my own art pieces for the Fire Arts festival while working on Soma. I remember Rebecca grabbed me by the shoulders at the Fire Arts festival. "Look at what you did. You said you were going to do it and you did it. You are a super star." To this day, she calls me Catie Superstar. I'll never forget what she said." Catie took off her cowboy hat and ran her fingers through her dusty hair.

I walked slowly back to my campsite after supper. Catie's story reminded me of back home. How intimidated I always felt around the better players in my music community in Boston. Some of the best musicians in the city had slept on my couch at Dustin Street, the musician collective I lived at. There would be people coming into town to teach a workshop at Berklee College of Music or some other conservatory in the area. We'd have visits from classical musicians who gigged in the New York, Boston, and Maine philharmonic orchestras and even Carnegie Hall. We'd have visits from folks billing stages at Bonaroo, and opera singers singing in every corner of the planet. *Why bother playing?* I'd ask myself.

I missed a chance by not being more open like Catie. I really could have learned everything I ever wanted to know about being a professional musician but I was too afraid. I wished I had fully stepped into the circle. Look at Catie now. She was leading her own art projects and became a badass welder in under a year. The virtuosity of everyone at Dustin Street frightened me when it should have inspired me.

Got to remember that...

Chapter 13

•

"A poem begins as a lump in the throat, a sense of wrong,
a homesickness, a lovesickness." — Robert Frost

It was Monday, and Burning Man had officially begun.
Thick traffic on Chaos Street moved steadily in all
directions, featuring a creative assortment of costumed pedestrians,
slow moving art vehicles, and cars packed to the brim with food,
water, and wide eyed people looking for a spot to call home for the
next week. Chaos was a fitting name for the kaleidoscope of things I
was witnessing.

I sat in my camp chair and perused the event guidebook as
the sleepy Burners in tents around me began to wake up. My finger
flipped it open to Monday and I searched for some fun stuff to do
before my evening fire safety shift: Fishbug's debut at Burning Man.

Each event was labeled with a particular symbol to identify
the type of activity. There were symbols for food, services, kid-
friendly events, drinking, lectures, classes, games, spiritual events,
rituals, community, and adult. You could find almost anything you
wanted or didn't even know that you wanted to do in that book.

Light gusts of sand blew in from off the playa as I made my
way through the thick Esplanade traffic. Bikes wove around each
other at a steady pace. People smiled as they walked past one
another, saying hello simply for the sake of saying hello. Good
vibrations were absorbed by the ground with every step and
seemed to effortlessly bubble up into the collective consciousness.
People walked steadily along in colorful, sometimes humorous,

ornate dresses or in the nude. I saw a guy wearing a t-shirt and no pants. Burners like him were called "shirt-cockers."

I made my way down Nine O'clock toward the Pancake Playhouse at the circle plaza. I peeked behind a curtain and saw people inside busily pouring pancake batter on a hot griddle, surrounded by mountains of pancakes.

A bell rang and a shade pulled up to reveal a counter and a kitchen behind it. A tall broad shouldered woman stood in the window. "Do you have a plate? Okay then, hold out your hand." She flipped a steaming pancake onto my palm with a plastic spatula. "Next!" she yelled.

"Ouch," I winced as I walked away. It was still burning hot off the griddle. I tossed it back and forth from hand to hand until it cooled. I then went to the syrup counter, and poured it on thick, accidentally getting my sleeve sticky too.

Pancake and syrup in hand, I plopped down next to a woman in a straw hat and light-brown hair. She wore a soft black sweater with a small globe brooch pinned to it. She spoke in a British accent.

"Are you just here for Burning Man?" I asked as I munched on my pancake.

"No, I'm on a world trip," she replied. "I'm just trying to figure out my life. I was a nanny in London but I really just want to play music."

"Why did you leave? You could probably just get gigs in London, no?" I asked.

"I wanted to see the world. Get some inspiration. I miss my boyfriend so much though. It's so sad to leave people you love," she added.

"It can be tough leaving your home." I felt a little sad just thinking about it.

We continued our conversation and became more and more nostalgic. As if on cue someone turned on a John Denver song.

My bags are packed I'm ready to go.

"Perfect timing." Jenna smiled.

I hate to wake you up to say goodbye.

A guy by the radio turned up the volume, and Jenna began to sing along to the recording. Others joined in with her. Soon every syrupy-handed person at the Pancake Playhouse was singing, some with their mouths full and singing only half the right words. I observed a piece of chewed pancake fly out of a tenor's mouth.

Leaving on a jet plane. Don't know when I'll be back again. Oh, babe I hate to go.

"That's so perfect," she said wiping away her tears.

Jenna left after our John Denver sing-along and I stayed to finish the last bite of my pancake. Hearing it made me think about my home. A home I lost.

*M*om and Gram had their system down to a science for making the best pancakes. The counters would be filled with bowls, wooden spoons, egg beaters, and measuring cups. The ingredients came out next: an open jar of flour, a carton of eggs, a small bottle of vanilla extract, and some milk. They never got too crazy with toppings, but I liked it that way. Simple was fine with me. I remember watching the square cast-iron griddle over the blue flame of our gas stove. How Mom would flick a little water on it to check for heat. If it boiled, it was time to ladle on the batter.

I know everyone's biased about how good their mom's pancakes were as a kid, but I swear, my mom and gram made the absolute best pancakes. They were always perfectly browned on both sides; insides cooked to perfection. Not too hard and not too soft. Those cakes made the whole three-story Colonial smell like breakfast heaven.

Gram and Papa's house sat near the top of Clyfton Street, only 2 blocks from Plymouth Harbor. From the hillcrest I could see and smell the Atlantic Ocean. All day long I heard foghorns blowing from boats leaving the docks. The house was covered in retro yellow and pink vinyl siding. Every year, green awnings were put up to keep the house cooler and taken down before winter. A long, patched cement driveway ended at a garage filled with ancient tools, bags of fertilizer, and scores of plastic gallon jugs of rainwater.

Through a white picket fence in the backyard, you could find Papa Mac most mornings tending his garden. To him, gardening was a science to be perfected and each growing season was a chance to do a better job than the year before. Red, yellow, and green peppers ripened during the hot humid summers. Juicy red beefsteak tomatoes hung from vines strung to long poles in the ground. Butternut squash, broccoli, bright green heads of lettuce, eggplant, peas, onions, kale, cabbage, and cucumbers came to life out of the rich black soil. My contribution to the plant life was my own cherry tomato plant, a carrot crop, and defending the garden from squirrels and blue jays with a pump action bb gun.

Inside 17 Clyfton was a thick red carpet and sturdy wood furniture throughout the house. A worn out cutting board sat next to my grandfather's faded grey chair, where he played game after game of Solitaire. That is, until we got a computer and he realized that he no longer had to shuffle.

Politics was Papa's strongest passion. He'd sit and watch bill after bill of legislation on C-SPAN's TV coverage of the House floor of Congress. We'd watch the vote tally one by one and celebrate if a bill passed that he liked. If it didn't go his way, we'd all hear about it. At one point Gram got the idea to buy Papa a foam brick to throw at the TV when he was pissed.

Papa was a proud member of the GOP. For a number of years, so was I. I was so brainwashed by the right wing media streaming on our airwaves that I went as far to name my hamster after the Republican revolutionary, Newt Gingrich. "Newt" for short. Howie Carr and Rush Limbaugh were on the radio by his ear and by proxy, all of our ears during every supper. Papa Mac would probably roll over in his grave knowing who I vote for today. I'm sure he'd blame it on the "left wing" media and my years in college.

Papa was also one of the hardest working guys I had ever known. He was a glider pilot in World War II, saved by Harry Truman's (or *Give em hell Harry* as Papa called him) order to drop the A bomb. He was about to fly a mission into Japan and probably would never have come back from that trip as the military were expecting huge casualties.

His philosophy was that you don't half ass anything. Every A on my report card earned me a buck. A B+ got you nothing but a disappointed look. "Hassan," Papa would say with his hand on my shoulder, "it's not doing what you like to do, but liking what you have to do."

Gram's armchair, covered with cigarette burns, sat across the room, but slightly more pointed at Papa's seat than the TV. From there she would do crossword puzzles and watch QVC, occasionally bickering with Papa.

The bickering was most prevalent when Papa got worked up about golf. "I've got to sit here and watch Tiger Woods scratch himself, while there are a dozen other golfers making shots."

"I'm proud of that young man, Harold. He's worked hard to get that good!"

If Sara or I were upset she'd tell us: "Hear no evil, see no evil, and speak no evil," and cover her ears, eyes, and mouth. Such a gentle soul Gram was. She loved my sister and me so much.

When I started playing guitar, I'd sit on her footstool and strum chords and half songs to her absolute delight. She always loved music and was so encouraging when my sister and I played. She was actually an opera singer before marrying Papa. Every once in a while I'd hear her hum the most beautiful sounds as she went about her day.

Everything about that home changed when Gram died. I was sixteen when it happened and it felt like losing a mother. She was the rock that held us together. I had only seen Papa cry twice, once when my Uncle Charlie died, and then once when Gram died. Papa let his incredible garden go to seed. Weeds took the place of ripe vegetables and the grass and shrubs got out of control. He was a lost soul after losing his partner of 50 years. My grandfather died only a few years later of a broken heart.

If losing Gram and Papa weren't tragic enough, seeing the rest of the family fall to chaos was absolutely terrible. Shortly after they both passed my aunts and uncles had a dispute over their share of the inheritance. The arrangement made between my mom and Papa was that she would get the house in return for being my grandparents' caretaker as they got older. She had to do much of the cleaning, grocery-shopping, take them to doctors' appointments, and anything else they needed.

My uncles would probably tell you that meant free rent. They didn't see what I saw. My mom had to work so hard taking care of them, all while working full time doing the books for M&M Sporting Goods, the family sporting goods store Papa started 50 years prior. On top of that she was a single mom raising two kids.

For some reason, Papa never followed through with his commitment to my mom. When he died, it was still written in the will that the house was to be split seven ways between the seven kids.

They eventually decided to sell Gram and Papa's home, which meant Mom, Sara, and I had to move. The only sibling who gave up their portion of the money from the sale to my mom was my Aunt Mary. "That was always Anne's money," she'd say. My mom was 55 and had to start paying toward a brand new mortgage. We lost our home and our family at the same time.

I can still remember one of my aunts walking in with a young couple and showing off the house like a piece of meaningless real estate. "You'll see a gorgeous sunset through this window every evening." I lived there my whole childhood and never noticed the sunset she was talking about.

The whole ordeal widened the hole in my heart. Driving by and seeing different cars in the driveway still feels off, as if there are people trespassing my house. It's not my house though and Plymouth will probably never be a place I'd call home again. I've missed 17 Clyfton Street, Papa, and Gram ever since. I've missed the feeling that I belong to an extended family. *It feels like the only family Mom, Sara, and I have ever had.*

Chapter 14

*"A house is not a home unless it contains food
for the mind as well as the body."* — Ben Franklin

The sun was high in the sky as I biked to the
Esplanade. I saw the road that led to The Man at the
center of Black Rock City, and realized that despite all I'd done so
far, I hadn't ridden up close to The Man yet. I was going to remedy
that immediately.

Once I was close enough, I dropped my bike and looked up.
The Man's wooden skeleton stood high in the air on a long piece of
lumber shaped like a Y. His body was surrounded by a structure

that looked like a fortress, constructed with nailed together two-by-fours. The Man's face was the frame of an upside-down pyramid, giving me a chance to put my own meaning into the void.

I began to visualize the structure's eventual fate, engulfed in smoke and flames. How could someone destroy something they had worked so hard to create? It must have taken thousands of unpaid hours, and months of hard labor to build the towering statue. Maybe to make something just to burn it forces you to appreciate the journey, because that's all you have. *Learning to let go.* Questions and ideas filled my head as I rode off into another dust storm.

I pulled up to Fishbug a little later. As I got closer my nose began to pick up the pungent aroma of marijuana.   "That is some strong shit." I heard someone say before collapsing inside Fishbug's stomach.

"What the fuck man? Are you ok?" another voice asked.

"Yeah bro. Don't move me. I feel sooooo goooood."

I poked my head into the stomach of the bug and saw two red-eyed stoners taking hits on a bong. They didn't notice me.

"Is it safe to buy weed from strangers on the Playa?" Stoner One asked from his spot on the hammock Gary had set up earlier that day, dangling inside Fishbug's stomach. He wore a pair of red and yellow striped trunks with a silver cape wrapped around his shirtless torso. A pair of mirrored aviators were propped on top of his head.

"Of course it is. And they're not strangers. They are just new friends with weed, man," Stoner Two answered back. They both burst into laughter. Stoner two had a darker complexion. I assumed he had left his cape somewhere, as they seemed like a partnership of flamboyant superheroes.

If they were anywhere but next to the highly flammable walls of the Fishbug, I would have turned a blind eye, but they weren't, so I had to say something.

"Hey, I'm sorry but you guys are going to have to stop smoking in here," I said firmly.

"Oh, sorry," Stoner One said, sounding a little embarrassed that he was too stoned to notice me walk in. "Ummm... Is this your art piece?"

"Yeah, I'm part of the crew."

"Oh, man, we love this thing." He sounded like Keanu Reeves from *Bill and Ted's Excellent Adventure*. They probably really appreciated a place they could hide out and smoke pot in.

"What is it?" Stoner Two asked me. "Is it some sort of elephant fish thing? It's creepy."

"If you put out the bong, I'll tell you about it."

The pseudo action heroes finally put the bong and bag of weed safely away in their backpack, yet a cloud of pot smoke still lingered in the air around us. I felt myself getting a little stoned just talking to these two.

"Yeah, so this isn't an elephant, it's a Fishbug." I gave them a brief description, their red eyes wide in amazement interrupting every so often with phrases like, "sweet, dude" and "cool, bro."

"Sorry to smoke in your bug, dude. We were just trying to get away from the dust."

"That's okay," I responded. "There have just been a lot of cops and Black Rock City Rangers making the rounds. I don't want anyone to get busted."

"Yeah sorry," he repeated. "Hey, we're just about to take off. Can we give you a gift for making cool art?" Stoner One wanted to know.

He reached into his backpack and pulled out a small plastic baggie, which to my surprise, did not appear to be filled with drugs. He opened it and took out a small twisted wire. The whole bag was full of them. "I built these," he said beaming with pride. *What were these two smoking?*

Stoner One held the wire up before him and sparked the flint on his lighter, then put the metal in the flame. The twisted wire quickly changed shape. It stuck up an arm and sprouted legs and a head. It was a miniature version of The Man.

"You can unbend it and do it as many times as you want," he explained.

"That's amazing,"

"Nice art, bro." They got on their bikes and rode away into the dust storm, with their superhero capes flapping in the wind.

I lay back in the hammock inside Fishbug and played with the wire they had given me. Fishbug felt so safe, I couldn't blame them for wanting to get high in here. It was a sanctuary from the chaos of Burning Man. It was my sanctuary now too as I lay down, embraced in its soft fabric innards. It may have been the first time in a long time I actually felt safe. Safe to be myself that is. I peered at the legs. I saw what *we* built. What the Fishbug crew built together. *A new home. It was time to let go. It was time to open my broken heart...What were they smoking?*

Chapter 15

"Every great dream begins with a dreamer." — Harriet Tubman

Whatt was supposed to be a short nap in the belly of Fishbug lasted well into the evening. I had a vivid dream of a Red-tailed Hawk soaring through a blue sky, chirping a beautiful song I could only faintly hear. It seemed familiar though. *What was the tune?*

I got up to the gentle shaking of my hammock by Poe who alerted me it was almost time for my first fire safety shift at Burning Man. Poe and I grabbed the extinguishers and the wet towels from the shed and dropped them in several key points around the structure.

As costumed Burners approached, they stared in awe at Fishbug. One by one, people pressed the flame effect buttons, startling the inattentive members of the crowd with bursts of fire. Thanks to the amazing fire safety experts on duty that night, no one actually caught on fire. And Michelle did smack about three people with wet towels: one of them was trying to light a cigarette on the left tusk and the other two were both on drugs and wearing what were possibly the most combustible fur costumes I had ever seen.

Hours passed and it felt like over a thousand people showed up. Wide-eyed pedestrians gathered around, and random art cars screeched to a halt to witness the spectacle. Hundreds and hundreds got to appreciate the bug that night. As far as I could tell, Fishbug was admired by everyone who crossed its path. I couldn't blame them. It *was* beautiful.

It wasn't till the late hours of the morning that the crowd thinned out. I walked over to Rebecca, who was standing alone by the fuel depot. "Congratulations," I greeted her.

"Congrats to you too. Thanks for all your hard work," Rebecca replied, taking a long satisfied drag off her cigarette and exhaling. She looked on at her work with approval.

Looking at the piece, I couldn't help but think of all the talented people who had put months of time and unpaid work into the project. They did it not only for the love of art and metal work, but also for the love of their friends. It was a proud moment for us all. *If Rebecca and this Fishbug Crew could build a gigantic Fishbug, what else is possible?*

My mind's eye turned inward to my writer's block. How long had it been since I wrote a song? How long had it been since I'd been able to look at my art with fulfillment? It was all I wanted.

I looked on at Fishbug. Glittering with fire. Its beautiful curves. The motion. The stillness. Its meditation against a canvas of chaos. My mind was still too. Intermingled with thoughts of my new community and my place in it. I was part of the Fishbug story and always would be.

I pedaled back to camp when my shift was over, through the sea of neon lights that glowed in the darkness. Fireballs and rockets from various art installations went off giving the crisp air a moment of warmth. Loud explosions rocked the night. I gave myself a challenge.

I will write a song at Burning Man! Maybe the Playa gods would listen and grant me enough inspiration to write a good tune. I couldn't go start my new life empty handed. I was exhausted yet at the same time rejuvenated. *Where's my muse?* I wondered.

Chapter 16

"Music happens to be an art form that transcends language."
— Herbie Hancock

I awoke the next morning to the beautiful melody of *Moonlight Sonata* being played by trained fingers on a near-by piano. Peeking out the door of my tent revealed a female pianist dressed like a Christmas elf surrounded by an attentive crowd.

She concluded the piece with a ringing C minor chord intercepted by raucous applause. "More music!" my neighbors shouted.

"I'd love to, but I've got to run." Her Christmas bells jingled as she pointed up the road. "Thanks for bringing this out here though. I'll be back!"

"You have a guitar," another woman called to me as the elf collected her things. "Come play for us!"

"Who me?" I felt put on the spot. My hands began to sweat and my heart began to thump steadily faster. For some reason the request felt like a threat.

"Yeah you. I saw you with your case the other day. Go grab your guitar!" she insisted.

"See, I'm kinda rusty. I don't know what I'd play." It felt like being called on in math class without having done any homework. I hadn't practiced in a while and had no idea what I'd even perform for them. I began to shuffle through the catalogue of worn out material in my head. I couldn't stand my repertoire.

"Please," she asked again with a warm smile. I wished Elf-Girl hadn't just played. That was a tough act to follow. That said, most of the guitarists I saw out there on the Playa barely knew even three chords on the guitar and even less knew how to tune the instrument, so expectations on the whole were pretty low.

"Sure, I'll play a tune for you guys."

I sat down on a stool and started tuning with one eye on the people lounging on blankets and soft cushions. Many had mixed drinks in their hands, probably stirred on the bar behind them. It only helped my cause if they were drinking. I considered pouring them all another glass of the hard stuff.

"Hey, is that a Taylor?" a guy asked from the cushion pile, snapping my attention away from my plot to booze up my audience. "You're a brave man for bringing that out here in the dust."

"It's all I've got for a guitar. I bring it everywhere," I explained truthfully.

I straightened my back and took a deep breath. My trembling hands reached for the first chord. My left foot tapped on beats two and four as the melody and lyrics escaped my shaking lips. My voice quivered as I sang the first line.

Grand Piano, designer hats, a pool house, Siamese cat, marble floors, she still wants more from me. Second job, overtime, maybe I'll turn to a life of crime, all in all to keep my baby satisfied. I noticed them tapping to the rhythm.

I struck on the last chord repeatedly and my heart pounded. To my surprise, they cheered wildly despite the many errors I had counted.

"You're good, man! Play some more," they demanded.

"More huh? You guys are relentless!" Their enthusiasm surprised me. Fueled by their corroboration I played almost a full set.

"Come back any time," called a gentleman from a folding camp chair. "We love live music." He then presented me with a bottle of red wine made from his vineyard in Napa Valley as a gift. *True Blood* was written on the label.

Just as I was about to leave, a guy walked in off Chaos Street, carrying a banjo. A cloud of dust rolled in behind him like we were in an old western movie.

"I heard you playing as I was walking by. Do you want to pick one quick?" *My god. Will this end?* My stomach tightened.

All the eyes in the shade structure waited for my response. "Sure," I answered, gulping down what felt like a sour frog.

"Do you know any old-time tunes?" he asked, twisting his tuning pegs.

"How about *Angeline The Baker?*" That was one of the first traditional tunes I ever learned, and it only had two chords. His fingers flew across his Goodtime five string. The audience began clapping to the beat.

Angeline the baker, Angeline I know. I should have married Angeline, twenty years ago. The audience applauded enthusiastically.

"Pickers!" called a random guy from the opposite entrance. The middle-aged man eyed our acoustic instruments approvingly. "Hey, you've gotta come play for us next. I play the mandolin and my friend plays fiddle. We've got ourselves a band! You're the first banjo player I've seen at Burning Man this year. Quick question. What's the best pick-up to put on a banjo?" The banjo player shook his head, knowing where this was heading. "A Ford F-150!" he howled from the corner. The joke got a mix of boos and hard laughs from the room.

The banjo player laughed too and did a quick finger roll for musical relief. "If we had a bass player, we'd be bon-ah-fied! Whewie!" he shouted.

"Just so you know what you're getting into, it actually just turned into an engagement party, so pick it hot." The mandolin player grinned.

We walked around the corner and quickly found ourselves under another canopy constructed from an old army parachute. People lounged on faded couches, beverages in hand all watching their friend on one knee proposing in front of a blushing woman. He slipped a ring on her finger and stood up to hold his future wife. They began to kiss as the onlookers shouted and whistled.

"Okay, guys, let's pick one," he said urgently.

"What do you know?" I asked.

"How about Wagon Wheel?" he offered. "She loves that one."

"Sure," I quickly adjusted the tension of a few out of tune strings in preparation. I thought about my bluegrass buddies in Boston and how they would be rolling their eyes at having to play this overplayed song. I took a look at the huge room and cleared my throat again. I felt nauseous as I began to strum. The bride to be smiled at me.

This moment is about them and not me at all, I thought to myself just before releasing the tunes first syllables. *Just play it man.*

Headed down south to the land of the pines, thumbing my way down to North Caroline. Staring up the road, pray to God I see headlights. The couple smiled at us and proceeded to dance.

Rock me mama like a wagon wheel, rock me mama any way you feel. Everyone joined in with the chorus. *Rock me mama like the wind and the rain, rock me mama like a southbound train. Hey mama rock me.* Our voices twined in harmony.

I repeated the progression and gave the musicians a couple extra solos. I also repeated the chorus a few extra times at the end so they could dance a little longer. They clapped and cheered for us when we were done.

Without any hesitation, the banjo player gave us a mischievous look and counted off quick – one, two, three, four. His left hand flew up and down the fret board as his right hand did acrobatic finger rolls. It sounded like I had been transported to an old Flatt and Scruggs recording session. I recognized the tune, Gold Rush.

We picked tune after tune as the crowd grooved to our sometimes unsteady, yet fun and danceable, break-neck tempos. I sang any old-timey tune that I could remember at least eighty percent of the lyrics for. That might have been a generous statistic towards the end of our set, as I dug into the rusty part of my repertoire.

After about an hour and a half, it felt like my hand was going to fall off. It had been a while since I had played that much at one time. To slow things down a bit and to give my achy fingers a break, I went into *Angel from Montgomery* by John Prine. The bride-to-be stopped dancing and took a seat in front of our sandy stage. She started singing along to every word and smiled at her partner. He responded by running his fingers through her dusty black hair and pulling her in closer. They swayed to the rhythm.

Realizing this was the last song I could possibly play for the time being, I gave everything I had left to give. The mandolin player looked on at my chords while the banjo player played along in perfect rhythm. We were really listening to each other on this one.

Sometimes you play music and reach something beyond words. Some call it the flow. I don't know what to call it. It was one of those moments that we all live for as musicians though. It's like letting go of the steering wheel, but less dangerous. In a way, the music plays you.

Make me an angel that flies from Montgomery. Make me a poster of an old rodeo.

The bride to be had her eyes closed. She leaned on the groom to be and started crying as we played. Her dark hair fell on his shoulder as the tears mingled with mascara and streaked down her pale face. The two of them gazed at each other and drew in closer. It was obvious that they loved each other. That was plain-as-day. I got goose bumps down my arms and teared up a bit myself.

We finished and they all clapped. I put my guitar down and took a seat as the party continued. I felt content with what we had accomplished, so it seemed like a good time to stop. I also didn't want my hands to have to be surgically repaired.

The bride-to-be came up to me. "You guys just played some of my favorite songs." She glowed. "One after another. Can we give you some cake or fruit smoothie to go?"

We happily accepted the bridal offering and helped ourselves to the cake. While I was spooning fluffy white cake into my mouth, she asked me a question that almost made me spit it out. "Would you like to play at our wedding? We could fly you out to New York when it happens. We'd be honored."

I was shocked by her offer. "I can't say no to that. It would be an honor." I scribbled my email address onto the back of a random business card that was in my wallet and handed it to her.

My heart again beat faster but not from anxiety this time. This time it was from joy. The kind of joy that a musician needs to keep going against what can feel like pretty tough odds sometimes. The joy reminded me of why I loved music. It had been a long time since I'd been reminded of that in such a wonderful way. Music really just gives you the ability to communicate directly with another person's soul. That's powerful stuff anywhere you go. The music we created that afternoon created memories I'm pretty sure that couple and I will never forget. That's worth something as far as I'm concerned.

I floated back to my camp on an imaginary cloud. My soul was rejuvenated and oozing with good vibes from deep within the core of my being. I felt as happy as everyone I had been seeing in the dust for the past several days. So many artists, myself included, spend years searching for some deeper meaning to art and life. Maybe it's simpler than we think. Maybe it's about experiences like this.

Music is meant to be shared and felt in person. It's supposed to move you. My music helped that couple celebrate their love for each other. I felt like crying just thinking about it. What more can you ask for from music?

Chapter 17

"To walk safely through the maze of human life, one needs the light of wisdom and the guidance of virtue." — Buddha

I picked up the small event booklet off the floor of my tent and thumbed through the plethora of options. There were hundreds of different roads I could take that morning alone. *What would I choose?*

First I noticed: *'Introduction to Human Sexuality' at One O'clock and Adapt. Learn about sexual response, safe sex, self-expression, masturbation, non-monogamy and again, safer sex.*

Below that, the *'Evolution of Consciousness Through Tantra.' Learn to awaken your astral energies through tantric meditation, breathing, sound and movement.* Useful, but too new-agey for me I thought as I flipped to the next page.

'Lesbian Sex 101' at Four O'clock and Inherit. Sounded interesting, but they probably wouldn't let me in.

'Beer Fest. Compete for prizes in the Olympics of beer.' I circled that one just in case I was around Seven-Thirty and Adapt later.

The pages of random stuff to do just went on and on. Drumming Poetry, Beginning Yoga, Weird Underwear Brigade, Pole Dancing, Hunter S. Tuesday, Granny Panty Night, Rubber Chicken Social, Rebirth Ritual, and Towers of Shiva, to name a few. In the noise of options, I decided to throw the book in my back pocket and ride off. Fate would steer me that afternoon.

I pedaled by a shade structure at Center Camp with a paper sign by the entrance. *Free Spiritual Readings with Esmeralda Alonza.* I felt compelled to inquire.

"Can I get a reading?" I asked a young blonde in a camp chair out front.

"Sure, but you'll have to wait. Miss Alonza is with someone right now."

After some time, a woman emerged from inside the darkened cave, escorting a man back to the waiting area. She was dressed in a dark purple shawl with beads draped around her neck. Deep lines in her skin traced the bones in her face.

The man exiting with her looked unnerved. "Thanks for the reading Miss Alonza."

"You're welcome." Her dark eyes shifted to meet mine. "Are you next?" I was suddenly nervous. *Would this reading reveal something I didn't want to know?*

I followed the fortune teller through a curtain of beads and transparent fabric. A few cushions were scattered around the perimeter and a small round table with three purple candles sat in the middle of the dark room flanked by two benches.

"Come and sit down." She had already taken a seat under the flickering lights. "What brings you here today?" She dipped the end of a bundle of sage into the flame and placed it in a small tray next to the candles. Wafts of smoke filled the air.

"I'm feeling lost. I've been driving around the country and all these wonderful things keep happening. But I'm afraid. I feel like I'm being reckless. How can I know I'm on the right path when I'm not sure where I'm going?" The cloth shifted slightly and the flames wavered. She deftly repositioned the cloth, squinting to make sure it was perfectly aligned.

"Let's pause a moment and celebrate the path you *are* on, even if it's filled with doubt. Why let a moment of significance slip by? Focus on your desires now." She tapped a perfectly round meditation bowl on the table with a wooden mallet. A ring filled the air, breaking up the rhythm of the candle flame.

"Where have you been during your travels?" she asked.

"Over the past few months, I've seen a huge chunk of the southern half of America. Life is a mix of exciting, inspiring, tiring, up, down, and everything in between. Almost on a whim I decided that I wouldn't return home. For a lot of reasons, I can't go home. But now what?"

"Uprooting is one of the hardest things we can do." She pulled a small leather-bound book from the shelf. "When is your birthday?"

"October 27th, 1983."

"A Scorpio." She began flipping pages. "Very intense characters are Scorpios. Mars is your travel planet, and it's in flux right now. You also left during Mercury retrograde. It seems like things should be dramatically changing for you."

"A Mercury retro... ummm... ninth what?" I stumbled out loud. "I just got fed up with always being stuck. Always failing. Always hurting. Leaving feels right, but I'm not sure where to go. No job or job prospects, especially with the economy wallowing in the Great Recession. There are more dead ends than through streets in America these days. When Burning Man is over, I'll be forced to face that reality."

She nodded and tucked the book back into some folds in the tablecloth. "Well, try to answer it for me now. Sometimes, we simply need to try making a decision and let the rest follow suit. What *are* you doing?"

"Ummmm... I'm." I tripped on my words. "I'm determined to write a song at Burning Man. But I only figured that out about a day ago." I frowned.

Miss Alonza regarded me thoughtfully. "Scorpios." She giggled.

I continued my story and got to the parts that were more positive. My mood improved. I even explained the internal workings of the Fishbug. She probably didn't care how many flame effects were on the spine, but she appeared to be listening intently.

"And so here I am, huddled around three candles complaining to a perfect stranger," I finished. "What would you do in my shoes?" The candle wax continued to drip onto the table in thick gobs. The flames flickered as we spoke, moving with each syllable.

"Well." She folded her thin wrinkled hands together in her lap. "That seems like quite the trip. I think you already know what you have to do. If you go back to Boston, it would be a step backwards. You need to acknowledge that, and allow yourself to receive the gifts the universe is offering to you, some of which you have already received. The universe is trying to tell you something. You need to listen." She paused to collect her thoughts. "Ultimately, you have to make the decision on your own, but I feel you should continue the journey. When we use our intuition and have faith, life's door unlocks for us. The doors will continue to open if you continue to be open."

There was a long pause before she spoke again.

"I wish you the best of luck," she said, bringing our meeting to a close. "I feel you will find much of what you need right here," she added, picking up a handful of desert floor and pouring it back onto the ground.

"Thanks for the advice," I said as we stepped through the hanging beads and into the sunshine.

There were a few people gathered, sipping water and waiting for their readings. I flipped on my goggles, took one last look at the waving Miss Alonza, and rode out onto the Playa.

After my encounter with Esmeralda, the motivation for attending the Beer Olympics was gone. Riding around and mulling over what had just transpired seemed like the only option before my next fire safety shift at the Fishbug that evening. I could predict one thing for sure though: Smacking people with wet towels was guaranteed to offer me some clarity.

I made my way down the Esplanade and peered at the temple from across the Playa. That seemed like the best place on the Playa to match my introverted mood. I pointed my handlebars in its direction and began to pedal.

The temple was quiet when I pulled up. People walked the wooden planks of each floor in near silence. There were voices, but only whispers. This was a holy place.

I made my way to the third floor and sat propped up next to a railing overlooking the whole Playa. A cool breeze blew in off the mountains giving me reprieve from the dry heat. I observed how many more notes had been added to the wooden surface.

Truth is one, paths are many. Next to it was, *We are part of this earth, let's evolve together.*

I saw a man crying and scribbling down text on the railing next to me. I tried not to distract him as I watched, but he seemed totally absorbed in his own thoughts. I wondered what he was writing. His tears blended with the Playa, caking onto his skin. Drops fell onto the dusty deck of the temple. A tattooed woman noticed him crying and put her arms around him. The man cried harder as she consoled him.

I peered at the text. *To the makers of this temple. Thank you for this beautiful place. My son committed suicide this year. This building sets him free. I'll always miss you Charlie. Goodbye.*

As he exited to the lower level I couldn't help but tear up a bit too, thinking about his son. *How much sadness was there bottled up inside him?*

I began deeply observing the structure holding all these stories. I saw the *real* temple. What a beautiful temple. These wooden planks gave people the freedom to release their demons. The Temple helped people suspend disbelief and take a leap of faith. It made people listen to their heart and their gut. It gives a person the freedom to say, *let me do this even if I can't explain it.*

I noticed another bit of writing in black sharpie at my feet. *Don't stop what you are doing, and if you happen to stop, you'll just appear to do so. – Sasha*

Just keep doing what I'm doing. I thought about my meeting with Esmeralda Alonza. That's basically what she said, but I didn't hear it like I did now. It felt more like a piece of wisdom to embrace on the temple walls. It felt like truth. Staying open and riding things out *was* the plan. Giving myself permission to improvise. The East Bay was going to be my new home for a while once Burning Man was over. I knew that much. It was a start.

Chapter 18

*"A good artist should be isolated. If he isn't isolated,
something is wrong."* —Orson Wells

Stars began to flicker over Black Rock City. Glow
sticks and neon lights on the arms and necks of Burners
compensated for the darkness. I joined them with the click of my
headlamp.

Chaos Street was lit like a Christmas tree, glowing lights
strung on people and vehicles alike. People decked out in their
wildest attire flowed steadily toward the Esplanade for the nightly
festivities. The most peculiar was a party of a slowly walking group
of men and women on blinking stilts. Many were probably heading
for the free happy hours scattered at various theme camps, catching
art car rides or dancing all night to heavy electronic music.

My bicycle tires bounced erratically in the street's divots. I
tightened my grip to my worn handle bar covers and carefully
wove through the sand. At an intersection I saw a couple of people
bouncing ten feet into the air behind a shade canopy.

"Hey, do you want to jump with us?" a woman called from
the trampoline as I rode by.

I slipped off my shoes and climbed up after emptying my
pockets of keys, wallet, and headlamp. The two women on the
trampoline bounced and giggled. I jumped in close proximity to the
pink glow stick girl and sent her flying. She shrieked as she came
down. We erupted in laughter. After a few more jumps to get the

height I needed for a flip I kicked my feet back and landed a front flip. The girls whistled.

"Thanks." I slid off the edge and into my shoes. I picked up my things and rode off with a sense of accomplishment.

Speeding as fast as the dust-encrusted bicycle would allow, I made my way down Biology Street through a zoo of unkempt revelers. After a quick turn at the Four-Thirty intersection I heard a scream.

"WOAAAAAH LOOK OUT!"

I squeezed my hand brakes and cranked the handlebars to my right. My whole body clenched as inertia and momentum nearly sent me airborne. Our two pedal powered vehicles grazed each other in a near impact.

"You need some lights on you!" she scolded. "It's dangerous to ride without them. Here you go." She strung a bright red glow stick around my neck. "Be careful. People need to see you coming."

By the time I got back to the trampoline, the two women were gone. I did a quick search and made a frustrating realization. I needed a headlamp to find my headlamp.

I patted the earth and felt panic and sadness. The darkness engulfing my eyes highlighted a loneliness that was creeping up on me since I arrived at the festival. *What the fuck am I doing out here?* Nighttime can be very lonely at Burning Man but this was the worst so far. Music blasted in the background and everyone around me seemed totally wasted or in a hurry to go somewhere. My senses were overloaded.

My hand reached for my forehead as it began to pulse and ache. I missed my old friends. I missed the feeling of actually knowing the people I was with. My heart ached for some close companionship that could never be replaced with even the most open strangers at Burning Man. Who were these people glowing in the darkness anyway? It's ironic how sometimes the more people there are, the more impersonal the environment can actually feel. *I'm alone again. The guy with the hole in his heart.*

My mind drifted to the summer after my junior year in high school. I had gone over to a friend's house for the first time. I pulled into his driveway and walked through the front door to find his obese mom, dad, and aunt watching TV in the living room.

"Introduce us to your friend, Steve," his mother asked while lowering the volume.

"This is Hassan."

"Hussein? How do you say it?" Steve's aunt interjected in a crass New England accent.

"Hassan," I repeated, anticipating the question. Almost everyone in Plymouth had trouble with my name.

"Why'd you let the terrorist in the house?" his aunt shouted from the couch. My heart started beating fast. I looked around and all the adults in the room seemed to nod in agreement. I felt dizzy standing before them, wondering why these fifty-somethings didn't know better.

Steve glanced back at me looking half embarrassed and half amused. "Don't mind her."

"Watch out for Mr. Al Qaeda. We've got our eye on you," his aunt commented again.

"I should get going," I finally blurted out. I walked out the front door to the sound of muted chuckles from the adults behind me, knowing that would be the last time I stepped foot in that house.

I wish that was the only time something like that happened but it was more common than I'd like to admit. It was tough being the only Arab in a nearly all white xenophobic suburb like Plymouth, Massachusetts. Being of Middle Eastern descent basically puts you into second-class status.

High School gym class was probably the worst. "Hey sand nigger," I'd get called by the seniors. When they'd get clever they'd use names like Camel Jockey, and Dune Coon. At one point, a few of the seniors agreed my nickname was Saddam. Even people who I thought were my friends would joke about it.

There were only two Arabs in my almost all white school, my sister Sara and myself. Sara had been able to conceal her Middle Eastern heritage by playing up being Italian. I couldn't blame her. Being Arab was not cool and with a name like Hassan I had nowhere to hide. I felt like a pariah in a sea of ignorance.

The racism even seeped into my interactions with my relatives. None of my Mom's half Italian half Finnish side of the family could really even pronounce my name. They'd pronounce it like it was spelled Hasan, with a long drawn out A sound. Hassan is pronounced Hu- SUN. The enunciation doesn't bother me now. It just underlines a bigger point. My own family didn't understand my culture and didn't care to.

If my Arab relatives were around early on, I might have learned to have a healthy pride for my heritage. Instead, it was just a part of my identity I was mocked for. I had to figure out my own ways for dealing. How do you learn to have pride in your race when you were never taught how?

*E*xasperated, I gave up my hunt for the lost headlamp. I got back on my bike to be a shadowy peddler cruising though the glow-stick city. It was going to be tough to navigate the pitch-dark evenings of the Black Rock Desert without it.

As I pedaled away, I saw a peculiar bright white light in the middle of the street. The white bulb sat there, waiting to be crunched under a bike tire, or to be found by someone new. Maybe by some odd series of events that actually was my runaway headlamp glowing on the sandy street? I felt a flicker of hope.

I rode closer and got off my bike, but as I bent down to pick up the bulb it shot several feet away from me.

I walked toward the light and again it shot a few more feet out of reach. After turning like I was giving up, I launched into a full sprint towards the bulb. The white light moved quickly, skipping over the roads uneven surface as I bolted through the crisp evening. My lungs gasped for air as my feet pounded the street in pursuit of the speedy glowing object.

I stopped out of breath and panted loudly. The lamp stopped as well.

"HAHAHAHAHAH!!!" I heard hunched over as I sucked in as much air as my lungs would allow. In front of me stood a man who looked to be in his fifties, with a fishing pole gripped in his right hand.

"You did a full sprint!" he howled.

"Yeah I know. I was there," I said sarcastically. "It seemed like a good idea chasing a headlamp on a string," This obviously wasn't my lamp at all, just a gag I fell for hook, line, and sinker...

"Hey Fred, I caught one!" The fishing pole guy was beaming. "You look like you want some food." The guy was still laughing.

The still-steaming meat on the table, wafted savory smells in all directions. I hadn't had meat since I arrived and this smoky barbeque scent was testing my will.

"You gave us quite a laugh at your expense. I feel like we owe you one."

Next to the rack of ribs sat an overflowing salad bowl surrounded by bottles of dressing. I felt a brief moment of guilt. What would Camp Spontaneous Salad think if they knew I was here, eating meat? I was sure to have some explaining to do if they found out I was eating both meat and someone else's probably non-organic salad. My stomach grumbled in shame. I accepted anyway.

The three of them made room for me at the table and loaded my plate up with food. I fully appreciated every bite though I still wished I could have shared it with some old pals who I knew a little better. I was grateful for their generosity either way strangers or not.

I thanked the desert fishermen after finishing the meal. "Stop by again," they invited as I hopped on my bike. "You can come right up to our camp next time." They were almost in tears laughing at this point. I shook my head and rolled my eyes.

The rib dinner was a good find and I thanked them again as I rode off, but the lost headlamp still hung over me like a rain cloud. Even worse though, was that I really missed my close friends and family from Boston. All the while, the party raged on at Burning Man.

My thoughts shifted to my immediate task at hand. I had a fire safety shift to get to! Just thinking of Fishbug somehow perked my mood up a bit. I really did love that creepy beast. I guess things couldn't be that bad, if something that beautiful was my next destination.

Chapter 19

"It is not the strongest species that survives, nor the most intelligent who survives. It is the one that is the most adaptable to change." — Charles Darwin

I got to Fishbug and saw the flame effects were already lit. *PSSSSSSSSSSSSSSSSSSSSsssss,* I heard with each of Fishbug's breaths. The side panels expanded and contracted in steady motion against Fishbug's body, unfazed by the surrounding chaos. A heavy bass from a sound system nearby pulsed through the air. *BOOM BOOM BOOM BOOM BOOM!*

I tilted my head back and got a full view of Fishbug's brain, in the midst of broadcasting images of his internal thoughts for all to see. Fishbug was contemplating the flight of two sea birds swooping over an expanse of blue-green ocean. *Did Fishbug long to fly?*

"Hey Hassan, can you give me a quick hand in here?" a voice called from the scull of Fishbug. I went to investigate and found Poe teetering on a 6-foot green ladder planted inside the middle of the sculpture's head. A hand radio was clipped to his black utilikilt, crackling with occasional commentary.

"Hold the ladder steady." He fiddled with the projector mirrors in an attempt to get the light that cast images on the brain even sharper in clarity. "How does that look?"

"Leave it right there. That's perfect," I said.

Poe climbed down and a woman's voice came in through his hand radio. "Kshh. Poeslacker, Poeslacker. C.G. gofer, Poeslacker.

It looks like the DMV database is once again functional. We had a similar problem with the clone zoap instance getting hung up. I restarted it and we should be good to go."

"Ok C.G. Glad that's taken care of. And the Ethernet cable you were looking for should be in the drawer to your left." Poe responded.

"Ok, I got it. C.G. out."

"What was that call about?" I asked.

"Oh that was Camera Girl. We're part of the team that makes the web servers at Burning Man. We set up the microwave links bouncing off the mountains, creating the   Wi-fi hotspots out here. I'm also responsible for the database at the Department of Mutant Vehicles."

"I didn't know you could get Internet out here!"

"If you know where to find it." He grinned. "How does that image look to you now?" He maneuvered various levers on a small control panel.

"What are you doing there?" I asked.

"I'm operating the fractal imaging system controlling the dome's projections."

"Fractals?"

"Nature has a tendency to express complex systems with a simple set of rules repeated over and over. Much of Fishbug is also self-similar, so we decided that the theme of fractals should continue in its thought patterns." I looked up to see the blending of multicolored lights splashed on fiberglass.

"Kshhh. Poeslacker, Poeslacker gofer C.G. Where is that Ethernet cable again?"

"Sorry. I gotta take this one," Poe said to me while shaking his head and walking away from Fishbug to find a quieter spot. "Poeslacker here."

I took another glance at the head dome. The image of two birds careening over blue ocean flashed in the brain of Fishbug. Each new thing I learned about this art piece gave me a deeper appreciation for the intricate technical details of Fishbug. Her evolution was right there laid out in front of us.

Fishbug evolved to have an aquatic tail merging into a reptilian torso, which stretched out to its mammalian face, and finally its gigantic brain. Her brain represented the next phase of its evolutionary journey; heading away from the body and into a higher-level of thinking. Fishbug represented an evolutionary timeline. Her body helped inspire its genus name; *Chimera Sententia*. *Chimera* means, "mixed creature" and *Sententia* translates to "thinking creature" in Greek.

Fishbug had an amazing ability to adapt and grow from the challenges she was given. I envied her. Sure, the adolescent creatures on the primordial playground had a hard time accepting her, but she grew in the face of that adversity and found her greatest gift; an amazing sense of empathy and gifted ability to reason.

The 50,000 people out here at Burning Man were all evolving too, granted in their own unique way. Evolution was even on the damn ticket stub. If you weren't evolving out here, you were doing it wrong. I knew if I could just get through this rough patch, things would be better. My evolution would happen by overcoming the deep cavern of a depression I was stuck in. For the first time I was beginning to see the first rung of the ladder. I had to stop being afraid. I had to write. I had to be an artist. *Only a few more days to write my song. I've got to get moving. It's time to be a finisher.*

Chapter 20

"The world as we have created it is a process of our thinking.
It cannot be changed without changing our thinking."
— Albert Einstein

My eyes opened to the sight of misting breath in crisp morning air. My body shivered as I dangled from the hammock strung up in the belly of Fishbug, sifting through blurry memories from the night before. Birds flying, a late night cruise on an art car, a deep conversation with a stranger, opening up about Maya. *All a haze.*

The Playa was nearly deserted as I pedaled back to camp; the sound of my gears being the loudest thing I could hear for once. I passed a smiling couple cuddled for warmth, looking on as dawn broke over the horizon. I turned to look too. The sun was a scarlet orb slowly rising in the west against a backdrop of steep mountains. I breathed in slow and closed my eyes, letting my body be consumed in the warm light.

*P*ulling onto Four O'clock Street I saw the Neverwas Haul from the Shipyard parked near the road. One of its builders, Kimmeric, sat close by in front of his yurt attending a boiling pot of water. His thick Carhartt jacket was zipped up to his chin.

"Want some tea?" he asked while rubbing his hands together for warmth. He offered me a steaming mug. The warmth began to chase away the memory of the morning chill. "You're up early. Must have been a good night."

"Yeah, I'm still trying to piece it all together."

As we sat, an art car pulled down a side street, blaring techno music. BOOM BOOM BOOM BOOM.

"Pretty ridiculous huh?" Kimmeric shook his head. "Burning Man used to be a lot different. I've been coming here since 1991, you know."

"Was that when it was on Baker Beach in San Francisco?" I asked drawing on the little knowledge I had of the festival's roots.

"No, I wasn't one of the two million people supposedly at that beach." He grinned, holding an obvious note of sarcasm. "Everyone claims to have been part of the beginning. I don't know how many people could have fit on that beach though. Someone's gotta be lying." He laughed. "When I first started coming there were only about two hundred of us. By '91 we had already moved to Nevada. In '93 I started the Java Cow ceremony. I'd wake up early before the Man burned and serve everyone coffee."

"Fresh coffee in the morning is sure to make you a lot of friends," I commented. "How did you come up with the idea for Java Cow?"

"I wanted to celebrate everyday rituals. There is something grounding about having coffee in the morning. It is completely ordinary, but something we all do. It's a part of life that is taken for granted." He took another slurp of his tea. "I took some icons from the west: a cow skull and a cup of coffee just seemed to go together. Manifest destiny combined with the caffeine to fuel it all." He laughed. "Between fifty to a hundred people showed up on any given year. It was actually printed on one year's ticket stub." He paused for a slurp of hot tea. "That was a long time ago." A look of sadness filled his eyes.

"Why did you stop?" I asked, trying to dig a little deeper.

"I did it for almost a decade." He paused. "That's a little embarrassing. You know you have problems if you show up to a place like this for over ten years straight." We both chuckled. "I showed up one year and no one recognized me. The festival had grown so much I felt it had become obsolete. Burning Man swung in the rave direction. I guess it sells tickets, but at what cost? I knew things were different when I was attempting to carry out the Java Cow ceremony and some guy told me 'it's too early for this shit'. That was the last year I did it."

"I'm sorry to hear that." I said.

"It seemed like The Man was on a pedestal and I was just a speck on the landscape," he said plaintively, staring up at the morning sky. "Don't mind me. I just have an old guard mentality. I don't like the fact that this festival has gone from a spiritual experience to a gigantic party. I don't mean to sound too critical. I still come because of the art. That makes it all worth it to me."

I sat and drank my tea and decided to remain neutral in the touchy conversation. Something occurred to me though. People weren't coming to Burning Man to be someone new. They were experimenting with parts of themselves, parts of themselves that already existed. And when those pieces of ourselves get rejected, it hurts no matter who you are. Creating makes you vulnerable.

Kimmeric's story reminded me of my first solo gig in Boston. My first attempt at being an artist in a big city. The first time my art was so flatly rejected in front of so many people. I opened for a cover band called Buster Cherry. What a name! I don't think anyone clapped for a single thing I played all evening. I just saw a room full of disinterested eyeballs staring at me blankly. During one of my originals, *Unsinkable,* a guy in the audience yelled, "What is this, Care Bears or some shit?"

"This is about my dead uncle you fucking asshole!" I felt like saying right before smashing my guitar over the heckler's brainless head. *How's that for Care Bears?* Thankfully the night did not end in violence. But that was the last solo club gig I did in the city. Giving up seemed easier than failing again.

After tea, I went to my tent to relax and settle my mind. I lay down and perused through my event guidebook.

'Lil' Crackwhore Happy Hour at 4 p.m. Learn how to work the streets with professional Crackwhores.'

Then there was *'The Shirtcockers Ball'* at 5 p.m. *"Rock out with your cock out! Drink, dance, eat! Contests for best shirt. Ladies, join us for a laugh."*

I kept reading. *'Zombie movie night'* at 7:30 p.m. *Join us for a mid-week scare! We'll be showing Dawn of the Dead. Bring your own chair and bowl for popcorn.'* I circled that one in case I was near Three-Thirty and Fossil later. I'm always down for a good zombie flick, or even a bad one.

'10:00 p.m. Dance at the Fishbug. Come shake your fish feathers at the best critter on the Playa. Music and visuals provided by Camp Phage.' I had almost forgotten about the party later that night. My evening plans were settled.

As I relaxed at camp, I grabbed my guitar out of its case and began to play. Some words were on the tip of my tongue.

You and me got no other place to be so let's be where we be right now.

I repeated the line I had started back in San Francisco on the floor of my temporary crash pad. A vision streamed in my mind's eye as I sat hunched over my guitar. There was an ancient tree with twisted branches stretching high above me while its gnarly roots sunk into the grassy earth. A blonde woman was reading a book at the base, sitting in the one patch of light streaming through the leaves above her.

We could climb, the oldest tree we find, and like the branches intertwined, you could put your hand in mine you and me.

I jotted the line in my book and repeated the two lines together. It all seemed to fit. *Who is that girl under the tree? Do I know her?*

I looked down at the nearly blank white page and time began to slow down as I rested my pen tip on the white sheet, ready to scribe something else noteworthy. My heart began to thump faster and a low-grade panic set in. I hoped that those few lines weren't all that was going to get jotted down. Nothing else was coming to me except disconnected, spiraling thoughts.

What was going on at Fishbug? Was there some art you should check out now instead? Why aren't you focusing man? You made a pact to yourself to write this tune, so start writing!

The nearly blank page sat there in defiance. It was time to give up. I could not concentrate for the life of me as the barrage of negativity continued to slam me down. *Why can't I do this?*

Swaying in the breeze I saw the parachute tent next door. Only a few days prior it was the location of the wedding hootenanny I played at. A bit of light filled my heart through the darkness as I recalled the beautiful bride crying to my version of *Angel from Montgomery.*

I stood up in defiance and grabbed my guitar case and began to walk. *It's time to act.*

At the corner of Four O'clock and Chaos was a bright white canopy. I could see a small group of people lounging in camp chairs with their bare feet dipped in a large, 10-foot kiddie pool filled with water.

"Hey, guitar guy," a woman from the pool called with a southern drawl. "Come play something for us?" She was completely naked. Her full body tan made me think she either belonged to a nudist colony or had been walking nude around Burning Man the entire time she'd been here.

"What do you want to hear?"

"Anything you want. How about one of yours?" asked an attractive nude woman with thick red locks.

I looked up and felt queasy from the anticipation. "Not sure what this one is called, but here is it." My hand reached for a G7 chord.

"Oh my baby's hot and cold, she don't know what she wants, when she wants, or how she wants it no. Doesn't know her up from down, no she don't."

I finished and they clapped and splashed in the pool. The redhead laughed. "I think I know that girl. Thanks so much for playing. Tomorrow at noon, we're getting some people together for a jam. Why don't you join us?"

Energized, I continued my journey playing music for anyone who seemed open to it. I felt like a minstrel in a post–Armageddon sci-fi movie. The next performance was at Camp Fucking Yay. Every square inch of camp, including the people, was covered in bright pink. They even had tiny pink buttons pinned to their shirts to advertise the camp slogan. After playing a few Grateful Dead tunes they requested, I was showered with tiny gifts and hugs.

I roamed further even more determined. I played for a happy couple at Three-thirty and DNA. Next was for an old man wearing a Grateful Dead t-shirt at Three O'clock and Fossil. After that I played for a group of middle-aged women under a shade canopy at Three O'clock and Genome. Each performance fueled the next. Before I knew it, I was almost half way around Burning Man. I challenged myself. *Don't stop until you reach the edge of the city.*

My arms at this point in the trek were in agony from lugging the dense guitar case. Each step under the hot playa sun compounded the heavy burden.

My next performance was for a crowd on a parked art car by the side of Two O'clock and Inherit. "Thank you!" I heard a guy shout from its roof. The hot sun continued to bear down on me. I was practically dragging my guitar at this point. *Almost there. I can do this!*

After one last performance at One O'Clock and Lineage, I walked past the last outpost at Burning Man and collapsed on the desert floor. All there was in front of me was a wide open expanse of desert and a jagged mountain range. *I made it!*

I noticed behind where I sat was an inconspicuous book shelf. Jammed on the top shelf with a bunch of other paperbacks was Paulo Coelho's *The Alchemist.* I opened to a random page and read a paragraph.

Before a dream is realized, the Soul of the World tests everything that was learned along the way. It does this not because it is evil, but so that we can, in addition to realizing our dreams, master the lessons we've learned as we've moved toward that dream. That's the point at which most people give up. It's the point at which, as we say in the language of the desert, one 'dies of thirst' just when the palm trees have appeared on the horizon.

I flipped to the next page, and then the book was ripped out of my hands by a sudden gust of wind along with the low rumble of an oversized engine. Panning across my field of vision from left to right, I saw one of the oddest looking art cars I'd seen on the Playa so far, and that is not said lightly. The front end was an old truck that had been converted into a tank. Its sides were covered in wood paneling, and a dusting of green paint created a camouflage effect. A long green barrel extended from the front.

The tank pulled a massive trailer, the roof of which was covered by a huge paper mache wind sail. It looked like the top of an oversized Conestoga wagon but made out of old bits of faded newspaper.

"Hey, take a census," a guy said as he walked by dragging a barrel behind him.

The driver of the art car staggered out of the vehicle and headed in my direction. His round black goggles projected three inches off his bearded face. The front left pocket bulged in the shape of a whiskey flask, his breath confirming its contents.

"Lots to do, lots to do," he muttered repeatedly, pulling barrels out of the back and hoisting them over the side of the vehicle. "Be a pal and give me a hand up here, will ya? The sail is coming loose," he called to me.

"Sure. I'll trade you for a ride back to Center Camp," I said in mild desperation, thinking about the long trip I had to travel lugging my heavy guitar.

"Deal – we're heading that way anyway. But first, we gotta fix this sail." He began to make his way up the rickety ladder.

I looked up and saw the wind-sail rocking back and forth, catching the strong desert breeze. I rushed up the ladder and grabbed one of the loose ropes dangling off the sail. A strong gust almost sent us both airborne.

"Don't let go of that rope now, ya hear? Or you're walking back to Center Camp. I guess if you held on, you might fly back though," he called jokingly over the swirling noise of the wind. Or at least I think he joked; my grip tightened just in case. "Thanks, man. Sit tight. I'll get you back when we're done dropping off all the barrels. It may take a while." His free hand reached for his flask.

Once we got things under control, I took a look about the wooden platform. It was at least twenty feet in the air giving me an amazing view of Black Rock City. I marveled at the streets wrapped tightly around the Esplanade and the myriad art installations constructed all across the horizon.

The census delivery crew returned a few minutes later and tossed the now-empty barrels into the vehicle. The engine turned over and we started moving.

"Hey guys, look what that camp just gave me," said a man, climbing up the ladder, preciously cradling a glass jar of pickled eggs.

I couldn't help but laugh to myself as we rumbled through Black Rock City in an over-sized tank, the wind sail teetering precariously over our heads as we delivered the Burning Man annual census to the citizens of Black Rock. I shared my first pickled egg with a girl named Inferno.

I flipped open a census and thumbed through it as we swerved our way through the side streets of Burning Man. It was white and folded into three sections. I glanced at several of the questions. *Which best describes the area where you live? Are you an artist? What's your race?* I quickly penciled in 'human'. *Did you graduate from college? Sexual orientation? Do you vote?*

Employment? Current gender? Personal values? Religious views? Importance of spirituality? What are you seeking to manifest in both the long and short term? How often do you feel like an outsider at home? Does Burning Man feel like home to you? What attracts you to Burning Man? How did you get to Burning Man? How often do you feel like an outsider at Burning Man? Do you plan on coming back? What's your greatest fear?

I paused on that last question. *What is your greatest fear?* I thought about my writer's block. I thought about the ramifications of heading to the East Bay without a song. I thought about Maya. I thought about Sarah. I thought about Mom and Dad. I thought what it would mean to never fix the hole in my heart. I paused. *That's it. That's the fear that rules them all.*

I spent most of the ride penciling in the census. At the turn of Four O'clock and DNA the art car hit a rutted patch of road and bounced the trailer off the ground for a split second, coming down in a crash. My core shook as we swerved along the dusty street. *My new greatest fear.: this guy's drunk driving.*

Chapter 21

*"The word enlightenment conjures up the idea of some
superhuman accomplishment, and the ego likes to keep it
that way, but it is simply your natural state of felt
oneness with Being."* — Eckhart Tolle

When we arrived at Fishbug the party was
jumping. BOOM BOOM BOOM BOOM BOOM
pulsed a bass drum in hard-hitting quarter notes. My instinct was to
leap in the air with each one. Camp Phage's DJ stood behind two
turntables atop a high platform, one hand up in the air waving.
Behind him were strobe lights flashing at the dancing crowd.

I pulled my eyes away from the dance party to prepare for
Fishbug's flame show. Todd and I started our shift by creating a
perimeter in front of the head. One by one people hit the button to
shoot Fishbug's fire tusks. Usually they'd look back at me right after
with a childish grin.

After a couple hours, Gary took over my shift. I went to our
supply shed for a beer and saw Rebecca sitting alone in the
darkness. Her black top hat tilted back on her head as she puffed a
cigarette, thoughtfully observing Fishbug and the crowd gathered
round it.

"Have a seat, you." She patted the camp chair next to her.
"How's it working out for you here?"

"Pretty amazing place." I grinned while slipping under the
yellow caution tape around our work site.

"You seem to be right at home here." She flicked the ash off the tip of her cigarette and took a puff. "Some people can't get used to the dust."

"Dust is in my veins. I'm half Bedouin."

She laughed and took another drag, wafting more smoke from her nose and mouth. Fishbug's sides lit up as the laser lights shot from Camp Phage's techno platform. Bodies were grooving to the heavy pulse of electronic music.

"What do you make of this place?" I asked, cracking open a beer from the cooler.

Rebecca scratched her chin. "I had a Native American friend, a very educated guy; the year he came, the dust was just awful. One day, the two of us found ourselves parked inside his truck. The whiteout was so thick, we couldn't see anything out the windows. When you're in that position the only thing you have to do is talk, I asked him the same question you just asked me. He answered by asking me 'Why does the white man have to go so far to have a good time?' He liked giving me shit." She took another deep drag off her cigarette and exhaled a thick smoke ring. "It's sad but true. Our society has basically removed the possibility for having profound cultural experiences. It's been done almost systematically." A huge ball of fire shot from the front of Fishbug, startling the crowd.

I gazed at the hulking metal frame. "You know, I've been meaning to ask you how Fishbug came to be. How'd you come up with this idea?" I indicated the 37-foot fire art sculpture in front of us. "It's so… unique. I've never seen anything, well…" I cut myself off to let her speak.

Rebecca took off her hat and ran her fingers through her hair. "I wanted to give people a metaphor to think about where mankind is going. I sketched a lot of drawings before finally coming up with Fishbug. The brain suggests the next phase of human evolution. Man's next step isn't in physical evolution, but rather an evolution of the mind. Enlightenment, so to speak."

Fishbug seemed to hear her. The air pump let out a hiss and the expanded side panels contracted into the Fishbug's frame.

Rebecca smiled contently at her creation. "I wanted to put it into physical form to allow people to expand their own minds just by considering the metaphor. They are given the freedom to go inside and find their own meaning, thus bringing them to a place where they can consider their own metaphysical evolution."

Another gigantic fireball from a fully charged accumulator tank shot off and startled the unsuspecting crowd.

"So Fishbug represents enlightenment?" I asked in an attempt to clarify the meaning for myself.

She raised her eyebrows. "Not represents, but rather suggests. It's our job as artists to point humanity in the right direction. Where are we going? How are we evolving?"

I walked back to my campsite slowly that night, pondering our discussion. My mind couldn't help but wander underneath the glowing Playa moon, as I'm sure so many had before me.

I thought about Rebecca's point that the next phase of evolution was going to happen in the mind. People's inner landscape would be man's next progression.

I desperately wanted for my inner landscape to grow. That was how I was going to participate in this global evolution of consciousness. I wanted my music to help people rejoice, or get through a time of darkness. Music that helped people feel less alone in the world.

This vision I had in my head of who I wanted to be conjured a very strong image. He acted confidently and was strong willed. He made shit happen. He got admiration and respect from his contemporaries. Juxtaposing that with what I saw in the present left me far short of the mark. The current version of myself suffered from depression and couldn't even write new music. Where was the confident guy to make a music career happen? I wanted to get over my issues right away, but stumbling on them every time I tried to take a big step took its toll on me.

It reminds me of the guy who goes to a guru and asks, how long will it take to reach enlightenment? The guru answers it will take 10 years. The guy responds, but I will focus really hard and meditate 10 hours a day. The guru answers ok, 20 years.

I could have just told myself that the songs will come when they are ready and all I have to do is be patient and have fun in the mean time. Opportunities will happen when I am ready for them to happen. But waiting for things to happen falls dangerously close to the lazy category in my head. Why wait when you can go out and do something?

I've always believed that it was hard work that got you what you wanted in life. You had to get your hands dirty and hack away at what you wanted everyday. I always thought the best and most successful musicians were the ones who practiced their asses off and who knew the rules of music and weren't afraid to break them, the ones who networked like mad, and who are respectful and kind to everyone they meet. Musicians who made it fostered deep relationships with their communities, and were organized and determined to take risks in order to actualize their career. Musicians who made it didn't stop pushing themselves. Musicians who made it were hungry.

But I couldn't just will myself to stop being depressed. My mind was a hostile place where I was constantly under attack. Before Maya, music had been my meditation. It connected me to the present moment, otherwise known as the access point to all the music that's ever been written and will ever be written. Over the years things changed so much. *How did I lose something so simple? More importantly, how do I find it again?*

Chapter 22

"If any human being is to reach full maturity both the masculine and feminine sides of their personality must be brought up into consciousness." — Mary Esther Harding

By the time I made it out of my tent that morning, the sun had risen high above the mountains. Chaos Street was filled with Burners of all shapes, sizes, creeds, and sexual orientations, hustling past me on their way to fulfill their daily contributions to the city's collective ode to freedom of self-expression. *How would I contribute?*

I remembered the lingerie party on the agenda. It was going to happen soon thanks to my late start. *What did Cheryl say? Something like four, four, and four. The fourth day of the festival, at 4:00 p.m, at Four O'clock.*

After fixing myself a quick meal of warm keg beer, uncooked beans, and a slice of wheat bread, I was ready to go. A lingerie party at Burning Man was sure to be filled with surprises. Even better, I didn't own any lingerie so I couldn't be forced to wear any. Fool proof... right?

I jumped on my bike, ready to speed off, only to be thwarted. My back tire had completely dislodged.

"Are you fucking kidding me?" This time at least, I was prepared for the fall and didn't gash my hand like I had before. My still wounded palm just wouldn't heal. Jess told me that it was the fault of the chemistry of the alkaline content in the playa.

My neighbor Melanie in the RV next door laughed out loud at my misfortune. She was heavyset, with perfectly straight brown

hair that fell to the small of her back. Her blue dress fit her loosely
and moved with the direction of the morning's breeze.

"Having some trouble?"

"Yeah. This fucking bike is just... I don't have my tools out here."

"Bring her over." She pointed to a small cardboard sign in
the passenger side window of the RV.

*Bike Repair Shop – Bring your beaters and get a free tune
up. No complaining allowed. If you don't like my only rule, then
you can kiss my ass and walk.*

"It won't be a problem. It may take a while, though."

"What can I do for you? I feel bad having you go to all the
trouble."

"It's not a problem. Just play some more guitar out here and
we'll call it even."

"Thanks." I was starting to realize how valued music was on
the Playa.

For fear of being late to Cheryl's underwear party, I began
my expedition on foot, leaving Melanie to tinker with the bike from hell.

I hadn't been walking long on Chaos Street when I heard a
voice call my name. I looked back and saw a large portion of the
Fishbug crew, including Todd, Gary, Christine, Meena, and Fresh who
waved enthusiastically to me as they trekked along the dusty road. We
knew that it was on Four O'clock, but we didn't know the cross street. I
wasn't worried though... finding a lingerie party at Burning Man
sounds easy, right?

We all spread out on Four O'clock Street and asked anyone
wearing underwear if they knew Cheryl of our Fishbug Crew.
There were a surprising number of people clad only in underwear
so we had our work cut out for ourselves. Half of the gatherings on
the street seemed to fit the criteria of the party we searched for.

"The party is in here." Meena pointed to a tent bursting with
people on the corner.

When we arrived, the party inside was in full swing and
bursting at the seems with scantily clad men and women.

Underwear hung from every corner of the place. I easily slipped by everyone, due to all the silky textures I brushed against. Once in a while, a static pop zapped my arm.

"Meow, meow," said Cheryl when she saw me from behind the bar. She was dressed in a black nightie and police cap. Her right hand gripped a baton that I assumed was getting a lot of use. "So glad you made it, Hassan."

"This party is fully underwear... I mean underway!" I said with a sheepish grin. "That was a bad one, huh?"

Cheryl threw her head back and bellowed a laugh. "You've got jokes now!"

"Hey, you can't be in here with those clothes on," said Cheryl's friend in a scolding tone, noticing I wasn't yet completely embarrassed. She grabbed me by the arm and dragged me to a nearby dresser filled with panties. "You know, I think this would fit you. Try this on," she instructed as she held up a silk hot pink slip.

The lingerie–clad policewoman's eyebrows began to furrow as she waited for my move. I took another look at the rest of the party to give myself a moment to think about the ramifications of this decision. Miraculously, at that very moment it occurred to me that there was an unfinished task at another part of the festival, which desperately needed to be attended to. *What was it? Had I left my tent unzipped?* That sounds like something I'd do. My tent was unzipped and that needed to be taken care of right away, I thought frantically.

"I think we have to start slow with you," she said, shaking her head and folding her arms.

She held a black long–sleeved lace shirt up to my chest and a pair of shiny green stretch pants over my legs. *Not too bad,* I thought. *I could do this.*

After I changed, I slowly stepped into the adjoining room, about to encounter the Fishbug crew.

I felt my face getting bright red as I faced everyone and saw they also wore lingerie. They took one look at me, and we all started laughing our asses off.

"Hot!" Cheryl was laughing hysterically.

"Looks good," said Todd. He wore a tight pink lace nightie.

Gary, Rebecca, Cheryl, Todd, Christine, and I sat in our various colored satin and silk night garments bursting into hysterical laughter each time we looked at each other.

"Hey, let's get a picture of us," Gary laughed, glancing at me.

"Uhmmm..." I muttered. *Where was this going?* I didn't particularly want the costume on the record.

Soon after, we were standing in front of the photographer as he prepared his camera to take our photo.

"Put down your beers. Kids might see this," the photographer joked.

Without warning, Gary jumped into my arms and made a hysterical face at the camera just as the photographer took the picture. We watched it air develop and I laughed harder than I remember ever laughing. The photo is still in Rebecca's workshop providing entertainment – at our expense – to anyone who crosses its path.

After we'd had our fill of women's underwear, alcohol, and lingerie police, our posse migrated to Poe's camp a few streets away, where fresh noodles were being served. They did this every day of the festival around two fingers above the horizon. It was getting to be about that time.

When we arrived, a long line of eager people stretched out from beneath the Noodle camp's shade structure. Next to the canopy a length of rope formed a circle in the sand. Inside the circle were two people in the midst of a sumo-wrestling match.

"If you win, you get to go right to the front of the noodle line," Gary informed us.

I watched and waited. In a short amount of time, the winner raised his arms in triumph and jogged around the ring punching the air. The loser got in line behind Gary and me.

"Can I get the next match?" I called to the guy engaged in the victory dance. He was tall, with a wide frame. His red striped pants fit him loosely and he wore no shirt, exposing a thick hairy chest. He shot me a look as if he wanted to bury me in the ground alive. I couldn't help feeling a bit nervous as I crept into the sandy circle. My head came up to the same height as his chest.

*P*oe acted as our referee. "It's going to be a clean match. You win by getting your opponent to step out of the ring or by forcing any of the opponent's body to touch the ground, other than the soles of his feet. That clear?" Without waiting for a reply, he chopped the air in between us and shouted. "Hajime!"

The match began. We locked arms, pushing each other for ground. His weight caught me off balance and I almost went down. I planted my feet deep in the sand and used all the strength I could muster from my abdomen to keep from falling over.

His arms dug into both shoulders and I felt my feet clear the ground as I was tossed to the very edge of the ring. I heard the crowd gasp as I waved my arms, fighting for balance. He crouched down again and came at me in a full sprint. As he came close, I dodged his advance and pushed him from behind out of the ring and on to his overly arrogant ass. The Fishbug crew cheered. Poe rushed over and declared me the winner of the sumo match.

"Hey, we gotta try that again, man. I wasn't ready." He sounded a little embarrassed as he wiped the playa dust from his knees.

"Let's do it." I answered, hoping my win wasn't a fluke.

Again we crouched, tossed playa dust into the air, and began the match. He came at me and we locked arms. Unable to free myself from his grip, I found myself quickly losing ground. The edge of the rope circle looming behind me. He took a breath and I whipped my arms free.

"Go Hassan!" a familiar voice hollered.

I crouched low and grabbed him around the waist, driving up as hard as I could. The two of us left the ground and launched out of the circle. By luck, he hit the ground before I did, making me the winner yet again. The crew cheered wildly.

"HASSAAAAAAN! WOOOHOOOOO!" The Fishbug crew yelled.

I was ready to go claim my noodles. I walked proudly to the front of the long line. The crowd parted a bit out of respect and I was served some of the most triumphant Asian noodles I had ever eaten.

Chapter 23

*"Tell me and I forget, teach me and I may remember,
involve me and I learn."* — Benjamin Franklin

I walked away from Noodle Camp feeling satisfied on multiple levels. The sun was starting to sink in the sky, darkening my surroundings. Blinking LED lights began to illuminate costumed bodies along Chaos Street. My bike stood upright next to my tent, resting on its kickstand with a small note stuffed into the wheel spokes.

Hey Hassan, the bike is fixed. Let me know if it breaks on you again.

My soul felt warm as I read. It inspired me to grab a pen from my tent and scribble down a heart-felt thank you for her.

Sitting in my camp chair, I flipped open my guide book to the Thursday evening events page.

'Pool Party @ Shallow end of the Gene Pool. Mutate in the Shallow End for a Pool Party. Have a drink of pool water, sign up for the swimsuit contest, and vote for the shallowest.   4 p.m. to 7 p.m. at Martini Village.'

Next was the *Zombie Pub Crawl* at Extinct and Seven-Thirty. *'Join our evil dead army in a march through the Playa with surprise displays of terror. Meet at the crypt and be prepared to attack.'* That sounded intense.

Next I read, *'Blues dance instruction at Tangled up in Blues. Learn to dance with Madam Cindy and a live blues band.'* I was sold.

I made my way towards the blues tent to scope out the jam. The nearby sign for the club glowed in multi-colored lights, illuminating the dark red fabric of the canopy.

I stepped inside through a curtain and noticed a white-haired gentleman riffing on a piano, his fingers moving nimbly over the worn keys. A faded brown corduroy jacket with two leather patches on the elbows made him look like a professor.

A small band was grouped around him, stand-up bass, sax, and drummer. It seemed like the jam had just started. People continued to trickle in, no doubt drawn by the grooving sounds emanating from the glowing tent.

A guitar stand with a black and white Fender Telecaster rested adjacent to the piano. My mouth began to water. No one was playing it. The strings looked old and worn. Thick layers of dust had collected beneath the strings covering the shiny chrome-plated humbuckers. I'd always wanted a guitar like that one.

"You want to play that thing don't you?" The piano player grinned. "My name is Yuri. That's Jimmie and Mike. You're welcome to sit in. Let's try *Rock me Baby.*" I recognized the title right away. It was one of my favorite BB King songs from *Live at the Regal.*

"You kick it off if you know it." Yuri directed and gave me a head nod. I played the main riff of the song and the band jumped in after one twelve-bar cycle. The audience was tuned into our groove and tapping their feet. Yuri crashed onto the keys as he entered, riding atop the sonic waves of blues music.

Rock me baby. Rock me all night long. I want you to rock me baby, like my back ain't got no bone, Yuri howled.

Yuri made eye contact with me and I knew right away that it was my turn to take a solo. Trying to prove my worth I dug in so hard I bent into a wrong note. Yuri's eyebrow raised up like it was attached to my flat A string. He gave me a sharp look. The type of look that said, *I know you hit that note, and you know it too... so there we are.* I kept going, but adjusted my dynamics to both play with as much passion as I could, while keeping my licks clean and in tune.

Yuri smiled at my modification and jumped into his own solo when I finished. Every note he played was flawless. His right hand rolled complex bluesy triplet patterns outlining every chord change with ease as his left walked a grooving bass line that carried the whole ensemble and every dancer in the house. The crowd clapped and shouted when he was done. With another head nod, Yuri raised his hand on the last phrase of his solo and came down with a crash simultaneously with the drummer's cymbals.

"Sterling baby! Simply Sterling," Yuri said, looking at me. "What's your name anyway?"

"Hassan," I answered. "You guys sound great. This your guitar?"

"It is. Take it easy on her though. I don't have any extra strings." He boomed with laughter. The band laughed too. "Just so you know, tonight we're playing music for a blues dance lesson. See that pretty thing with the blonde hair? She'll be leading it. Her name's Cindy. Listen to her, follow the changes, and you'll be fine."

People continued to trickle into the room and onto the dance floor. When Cindy seemed satisfied with the number of people in the room she took the mic.

"Welcome everyone. Let me introduce myself. My students know me as Madam Cindy. Tonight we're going to work on how to dance to blues music and fortunate enough to have a live band here to help us. Let's give them a round of applause."

Turning to us, she lowered her voice, getting our attention without letting the dancers hear her. "Guys, when I give you the cue, switch up the tempo. Start at a medium pace and then kick it up a notch."

The dancers paired off as we prepared to start the music.

The bass player was noodling. "Let's start together Jimmie and don't play the 7th in the bass. I got it. Hassan, put an A augmented chord in the intro. And everyone, watch for the turnaround. One, two, three, four." Yuri counted off at a medium tempo and we jumped into a twelve bar shuffle in A.

The dancers began to sway to the beat. We traded solos after a full cycle, waiting for our next cue from Madam Cindy.

"Keep moving. Keep that beat in your head, one two three four, one two three four. Step left, step right, back step, and again." She gave Yuri a head nod for the tempo shift.

Yuri raised his right hand getting us ready for the change. "One-two-three-four." He counted off with confidence. *This guy is a pro,* I thought to myself in awe of how tight Yuri's band leading skills made us sound. He made it seem like we had been playing together for years.

Yuri chuckled as we finished. "You cats are solid senders. I thought for a second there we'd end up looking like the north end of a southbound horse here but good on you guys for keeping it clean. Class acts all of you." The whole band laughed along with Yuri and his catch phrases.

Class went on like this for what seemed like a good few hours. The band got tighter and tighter as the night progressed. Yuri's leadership got the best out of us and had everyone feeling great and sounding better then we may have thought possible.

When class was over, I headed over to where Yuri was lounging sipping a Martini. I wanted to thank him. I was so envious of his band leading abilities. He gave cues, kept us on task and in tempo seamlessly. The guy made it all look easy. I knew it wasn't. Being a bandleader is tough and Yuri was a pro.

"Thanks so much for letting me sit in on the jam." I sat down next to him.

"It's copacetic man. You're sounding great." He finished his drink with a gulp. "They make these drinks strong out here. I'm two drinks shy of being completely zozzled." Yuri bellowed a laugh.

"I was wondering." I looked at the floor all of a sudden

nervous to ask my question. "Do you have any advice for a guy trying to start a band? It seems like you've got it down."

"Step into my office, young Padawan." He howled. I think my question served as an ego boost. "I know this sounds obvious but before you do anything you've got to believe in yourself and the music. If you don't believe, why should anyone else? The next thing about being a good bandleader is you've got to tell people what to play, without telling people what to play if you know what I mean. Wink wink." He grinned. "You've got to corral your cats without over managing. Create a good vibe, with good bread, and good music and the good players will keep coming back. Everyone's got different skills they bring to the table. Find ways to get the most from your band but also accept who they are."

"It's a balancing act." I said.

"That's right, and no one's going to do more balancing or wear more hats than you do. Be prepared to do it all. And the more successful you are, the more it's a job. Other than that, your guess is as good as mine." He chuckled as he stood up and patted me on the back. "It's been real talking to you, Hassan. You're a good cat but I've got to go see a man about a dog. Keep working on your music and you'll find your band. You've got the chops." I watched Yuri stumble over to the bar and order a shot of whiskey. I inferred that zozzled meant getting drunk in Jazz speak. I laughed to myself at the brilliant, hilarious character I had just met and had the fortune to play with.

I walked back into the cool night air, thinking about what Yuri told me. *You've got the chops.* I remembered my first bandleader experience in Boston. A few friends of mine offered to be my rhythm section and just like that, I became a front man of a band. I wish it had come with an instruction manual.

I had been in Boston for about a year when I met my bandmates, Brian and Alex. Brian and Alex were truly amazing players so I was honored they wanted to play with me in the first place.

We rehearsed in Lower Allston, Massachusetts for about 6 months. We rented out our rehearsal space for super cheap and got what we paid for: four cold slimy walls surrounded by punk bands on either side of us.

I don't think we ever truly connected musically. The way decisions were made, it seemed like it was Brian and Alex's band; I was just fronting it and writing the songs. After 6 months of playing the same handful of tunes over and over, they sat me down one practice and fired me.

Brian and Alex tried in their own way to be really kind about it, and wrote out a 5-page report constructively criticizing my performance as a bandleader and musician. They sandwiched the critiques with compliments. The two of them really liked my songwriting and my singing but my glass half-empty mind really just focused on their critiques. They basically said my rhythm was unsteady, I had trouble finding and staying in the pocket, my guitar playing needed work, and I lacked focus at rehearsals.

Instead of giving me a clear direction of what I needed to improve on as a musician, Alex and Brian's feedback really just gave me an even deeper complex about my playing. I would fear my rhythm was way off any time I picked up an instrument, and that would pull me way out of the groove. And there is nothing like fear to kill your groove. I hadn't been able to work up the courage again to front a band of my own since.

I wanted to be a solid leader like Yuri was, holding down the vocals, chords, tempo, all while giving us cues on solo orders and dynamics. He was the type of bandleader who knew all the parts better than the people playing them. He made the whole ship steer. Every good band needs a leader and Yuri made us good.

I'm sure he kept the good players around. I had a lot to learn from someone like that. *Keep working on your music and you'll find your band.* That'd been the plan all along. It was getting close to time I did something about it too. Only three days left to write my song. *Now or never!*

Chapter 24

"Et tu, Brute." —Julius Caesar

Strong winds swirled play dust around the Raygun Rocket. The start of the Friday night launch ceremony was only moments away. People were gathered in the thousands.

I set my bike down near a dusty parked van covered with DPW stickers and locked my eyes on to the rocket. I pushed through the throngs to the edge of the perimeter as a deafening siren wailed through the night air. Hordes of people pushed to get a closer look. A tanker truck pulled slowly through the masses heading for the fuel depot. Painted on the side in giant lettering was *Rocket Fuel.*

Suddenly a voice came on over the loud speaker: "T minus ten minutes."

"Roger that."

"Fuel supply at 100%."

"How are we looking on the bridge?"

"Engine pressure stabilized. Over."

"T minus ten, nine, eight, seven…." The crowd screamed along with the countdown. "Six, five, four, three, two, one, blast off!"

A deafening boom erupted throwing me back. A series of loud cracks and pops filled the smoky air. I looked up and the sky was filled with bursts of fire works that fanned out in streaks of light. The explosion sent multicolored fireworks streaking across the night sky. The crowd shouted at the top of their lungs.

After the fireworks ended cigarettes lit along the perimeter. The night sky turned black again as everyone dissipated into the neon glow. I looked around and saw that nothing behind me looked as it did only moments earlier. *Where was the van I'd parked my bike next to... and more importantly, where was my bike?* Each step in the search seemed to get me further away from what I was looking for. *I wish I had my headlamp.* My head began to ache. *Who stole my bike?* My heart pounded as I searched in the chaos. I rubbed my eyes and had a memory I hadn't thought about in years.

I was 16. One day after school I walked up to my grandparent's house and noticed the door ajar. Handprints covered the glass window under which where we stored our key.

I threw my bag down and took the stairs two at a time, heart pounding. My room was a mess. My jar of tip money from my restaurant job gone. My stack of CDs gone. My paintball gun gone. My sister's room, trashed. My grand-mother's bedroom door ajar. Her jewelry box emptied and broken on her floor. We'd been robbed, and I knew who did it.

I called my mom and told her what had happened in one long sentence. She said she'd come home from work immediately and asked me to call the cops after I got off the phone. When I dialed, it occurred to me I'd never called 911 before.

The police got there before Mom. The lead officer wore a bright orange jacket and asked to see where the break-in had occurred.

Maybe I should have seen it coming but I'd been friends with Matt and Dre long before their transition to being jack-asses. I'd known Dre since the third grade when he was still just a chunky little kid with a rat-tail, taking big gross bites of peanut butter and marshmellow sandwiches and breathing them on kids at lunch, me included. Fluff to this day makes me nauseous.

After about ten minutes the cop informed us the prints were too smudged to do anything with. Matt and Dre had walked away clean.

The next day I spotted Matt at the cafeteria. I got up from my table and made the long walk across the lunch room, past the senior table, past the jocks and cheerleaders, past the Goths, past the freshman, to the far end of the noisy room. I glared at Matt in his eyes, burning with anger as the eyes of every kid in the room looked on at the potential showdown. Blood rushed into my clenched fists. "YOU ROBBED MY FUCKING HOUSE!" I boomed with rage.

"No, I didn't," Matt answered calmly. "Where's your proof?"

"DON'T FUCKING LIE TO ME!" My blood boiled as I glared at Matt's bony face, feeling the gaze of a hundred pairs of eyes waiting for our confrontation to explode into violence. Where *was* my proof? The fingerprints had been smudged and no one saw them break in. In a way Matt was right. I had no proof. What I did know was that Matt and Dre had been robbing lots of people, including many in our circle of friends. I also knew that these two delinquents deserved my hardest punc14between us a moment before the conflict detonated.

"Nothing," I answered back, knowing that my life would get even more difficult if I ratted.

"This doesn't look like nothing," Mr. Seiver responded. Matt and I stood there silent. "Well, lunch is almost over. Matt, why don't you head to your next class. You sure everything is ok Hassan?"

"It'll be fine," I lied. I could see Matt smirk as he walked away from us.

Matt and Dre were my buddies and must have seen me grab the key a hundred times. It was a deep betrayal from people I thought were my friends.

The pair even had the nerve to break into my house for a second time a week or two later. This time they kicked in the bulkhead leaving a broken hinge dangling from the splintered doorframe.

"Why are you hanging out with those losers, Hassan?" My grandfather asked me one day. His disappointment hurt worse than getting robbed. I had let Papa down.

Matt, Dre, and many other kids in my high school circle were headed down the wrong path fast as bullets. I'm one of the few who went on to college and actually left Plymouth. Eventually Dre got kicked out of his uncle's house and lived on the streets.

After the break in, the line between friend and enemy had been blurred. I wasn't sure whom to trust anymore. Thefts and beat downs became a normal phenomenon at my high school. One Friday night, Dre and his crew robbed another high school friend of mine, Joe, at gunpoint. Joe had started selling pot in bulk which caught the attention of every wannabe gangster in school. The gang pistol whipped the headlights on his oversized Buick and stole a pound of weed off Joe in Morton Park.

Joe was furious after the robbery and called his crew, which I found myself to be a part of. We all agreed with various degrees of enthusiasm to meet Dre's crew for a fight behind Benny's parking lot in North Plymouth on Valentines Day. I got there to find both Dre, with his hair slicked back with a pound of gel, surrounded by a gang of fifteen kids. I heard later that a few people were even packing heat. Joe's crew numbered about seven including me. Most of the jeering mob surrounding us seemed to be biased in favor of Dre's gang. The odds seemed stacked against us from the onset.

The onlookers created a ring around us with their bodies and roared profanity. Joe and Dre met in the middle and we all got quiet waiting to see what would happen. My heart pounded.

In a flash, the eye of the storm ended with a loud "FUCK YOU!!!" and Joe's fist hitting Dre hard in the jaw. Dre returned a right hand to Joe's temple. Other gang members joined in throwing punches almost at random. I caught one in the stomach. My friend Matt got attacked by three kids and backed up to his car and pulled out a baseball bat in desperation. The kids around him fanned out in fear.

I found myself drifting toward the edge of the circle of bleeding bodies. I hadn't felt like punching Matt at lunch and I didn't feel like punching him at what we later coined the Valentines Day Massacre. I really was a pacifist and spent most of the fight trying to pull people off my friends. I knew that Matt and Dre deserved a beating but my teenage mind didn't really didn't see the point. What would that have proved? They'd still be jackasses and they'd still have our stuff.

Eventually the cops showed up and we all ran off. Though the kids escaped to loot and plunder another day, the troubles for so many of them didn't stop there. For some, they never would. Dre died of a heroin overdose a few years after I left college and Matt is serving time.

The Valentines Day Massacre was around the time I started playing guitar. I poured myself into music. It was the only thing I thought about. Practicing music became a place to escape from the horrible people and events happening around me. It was something I had control over. Possibly the only thing I had control over.

I took in the whole blur of the electric glow before me. The bike was gone, I concluded. I cut my losses and resigned myself to being a pedestrian for the rest of the evening. The loss felt more like liberation than a betrayal. I categorized the mishap as an *accidental* theft as I strolled away from the Rocket. It was easy to believe that at Burning Man. Even if it had been of malicious intent, I almost felt bad for the thief. That crusty death trap of a bike would be someone else's problem now. Going on foot isn't such a bad deal at a place like this anyhow. It gives a person time to take it all in.

Chapter 25

"Old friends pass away, new friends appear. It is just like the days.
An old day passes, a new day arrives. The important thing is to
make it meaningful: a meaningful friend –
or a meaningful day." — Dalai Lama

I awoke to a crisp morning breeze inside the belly of
Fishbug, dangling in the hammock. *What happened last*
night? The rocket launch, lost bike, a girl, and a weird black and
white '50s film on etiquette and proper manners. A long
conversation with a bartender about relationships. My head began
to thump from a nasty hangover as I pushed deeper into its caverns
of short-term memory.

"Morning, Hassan. Rough night?" Rebecca and a few of the
crew chuckled at the sight of me crashing in Fishbug. I rubbed my
eyes. Staring at me stood a bunch of the crew: Rebecca, Fresh, Jess,
Don, Gary, Mathew, Cheryl, Meena, Matilda, and Poe. I could hear
more voices surrounding the walls of Fishbug. Gary handed me a
bottle of Jess Lube – our name for Jim Beam whiskey, primarily due
to its ability to get Jess in a looser state of mind.

"Breakfast for Hassan!" Gary bellowed with laughter.

I got up and we all began preparing for the Fishbug flame
effect show. Rebecca stood by the fuel depot and switched on the
tanks. Gary turned on the air compressor while I stood by the tail
and turned on the linear actuator. Mathew stood ready with the
propane torch and lit the spine as Fishbug's side panels expanded
and contracted.

When we were done, I gazed at Fishbug and everyone around it. *Friends,* I thought. Gary brought out his six-string guitar and began to play as we enjoyed flame effects and lukewarm whiskey. The crescent moon hung in the sky like a crooked smile of the Cheshire cat just above the eastern mountains.

"Hey Hassan, what do you think of this Ibanez?" Gary asked. I took it from his hands and started a Travis picking pattern. My thumb alternated the root and 5th of each chord on the lower strings as my other fingers plucked out a simple melody. "It sounds like angels when you play man. I just tinker with the thing." Gary sat in the cool playa sand completely engaged as I strummed. "Would you maybe give me some lessons when we get back to the East Bay?"

"Of course, I'd be honored. Say the word." His kind words moved me. It hadn't occurred to me til then, but lessons could earn me money when we arrived back to the East Bay jobless and broke!

A peacefulness filled the air as the sun steadily climbed into view. So much of what I needed might already be right in front of me. The synchronicity was beautiful.

*S*tarting to feel the effects of breakfast, I stumbled my way over to the fuel depot for a break from fire safety. A blonde was sunk deep in one of the camp chairs, sipping a morning PBR. I vaguely remembered her from the Shipyard. A straw hat covered her curly blonde hair and shaded her distinctly Aryan features.

"Hey, I'm Hassan." I introduced myself.

"I'm Lara. How are you?" She eyed the bottle of Jess Lube in my right hand.

"You know." I grinned at her foolishly. Morning whiskey breath probably wasn't the best combination.

"What are your plans after all this?" she asked me. I suddenly felt nervous. It was hard to admit to people that I didn't have much of a clue. But there was a non-judgmental air to her tone.

"To be honest, I've no idea. I was going to look for a place in the East Bay. I'd like to keep learning about metal work too. And keep working on my music."

"Cool. What did you do for work before you met up with us?"

"I taught special education, and performed music with a few folk acts back in Boston."

"So not much background in metal work huh?"

"Not really. Working with kids has helped me out on some of my fire safety watches, though." I laughed and hiccupped simultaneously. "What do you do when you're not building Fishbug?"

"I do PR for an investment firm. Corporate slave work," she answered heavily. Lara took another swig of her PBR as flames shot out of the Fishbug.

"Not into it, huh?"

"No. I'm looking for something a bit more gratifying. Fishbug helps. This type of communal art work is so far removed from my responsibilities at work."

"I bet. I've spent most of my professional life in a classroom. I recently got laid off, hence the nomading."

"Yeah, Rebecca's told me a lot about you." Lara leaned forward in her chair and looked at me intently. "This may sound weird but I think we can help each other. You need a place to stay, and I need a subletter. I've got a place in Oakland. It's really close to the Shipyard too, if you are looking to spend more time there. Are you into dogs at all? You'll love Huck, my Bluetick Coonhound."

Another poof went off by Fishbug as a Magic Carpet art car whizzed by bumping Jimmy Buffet's tune *Margaretville*. A guy in a fez and a breezy red silk robe operated the steering wheel from the center of the carpet. The line of people at the poofer button began to dance.

"I need a bit of work done on the place. We could call that rent for the first month. I'm painting and fixing it up a bit. Simple stuff really, but there's a lot of it, and I could use some help."

"That's an amazing offer," I responded, breathless and woozy from the newly opened floodgates of possibilities. *Did I hear her right?* My heart pounded with excitement. I quickly racked my brain for the array of subpar options I had when I got back to town.

I saw a couch at the Shipyard with shrieking grinders serving as an alarm clock. My brain rattled from just imagining it. I could feel the metal dust coating my nose and throat like the playa dust had for the past week. That just wouldn't work.

I pictured my Chevy parked along pedestrian walkways in residential neighborhoods of crime-filled Oakland, me squished into the back seat getting woken up by loud pops from nearby gun battles or the light of a police officer's flashlight shining through my fogged-up window. That sounded like an even worse plan.

Next I pictured driving aimlessly up the coast and eventually retreating back to Boston; retreating back to a place that had been nothing but hostile to me from day one. I'd be jobless and apartmentless and playing for a band without a clear business plan. I'd most likely get stuck in the same muddy rut that brought me out on this blurry vision quest in the first place. The same rut that brought me to Big Sur. I might have to admit to myself that being a musician wasn't my calling once and for all. I might have to give up my dream. *HELL NO!*

"I'll take it," I blurted out. "At least for the first month. I love dogs and I'll learn to love home maintenance." It felt like a boulder had been lifted from my shoulders. Overwhelming relief overtook me as the images of my other potential fates faded into a fuzzy vision of a stark white apartment in Oakland, California, a saggy-skinned hound dog, and Lara, a blonde corporate powerhouse looking to help out a modern day nomad.

Michelle's description of ocean blue splashed into my mind's eye. Maybe I wasn't going to be sailing around the world, but I was seeing colors of life I knew I couldn't have experienced if I'd stayed in Boston. All of these unique, exquisite moments were breathing life into my spirit in its time of need. That much was crystal clear at a moment in my life when clarity was in short supply. I had the ground for music to start.

Out of the corner of my eye, I saw three giggling women chasing Gary around the tail of Fishbug with a wet towel. The sleepy monster continued to breathe steadily, observing us calmly in the cool morning. The projection system in Fishbug's bulbous fiberglass brain flashed images of birds soaring through a clear sky over an expanse of blue ocean. I had a place to live now. I still had to write my song, and much was still in the air, but sometimes you have to appreciate the small gifts life offers if you are open to receive them. *Thank you Lara, and thank you ebb and flow of the universe. Maybe you've been looking out for me all along.*

I raised the jug of Jim Beam and clinked Lara's can of PBR. We both took a sip and sealed our verbal agreement with lukewarm alcohol in the middle of the Black Rock Desert under a rising sun and a fading Playa moon.

Chapter 26

"Travel is fatal to prejudice, bigotry, and narrow-mindedness."
— Mark Twain

After Fishbug's dawn show I glanced across the Playa and felt a pang of sadness. Later that evening a spark at the base of The Man would turn into a massive fire and turn the wood structure into hot coals and ash. The festival's centerpiece would be gone and the last two days of Burning Man would blow by like a gust of playa wind.

A short walk across the Playa brought me to a tent called Muhammad's right off the Esplanade. The structure was about twenty feet across and ten feet to the back wall. The brown fabric was supported by thick wooden beams and staked with ropes. An ankle high coffee table covered in a blue and white star patterned tablecloth stretched the tent's entire length. Costumed Burners lounged on plush multicolored cushions and blankets, sipping mixed drinks in martini glasses. In the center was a gold and blue hookah with three checkered hoses and a bright glowing coal at the top. Smoke wafted upward and collected near the ceiling.

"Care for a Margarita?" inquired the host.

The vibe at Muhammad's was relaxed. I sat back and took occasional puffs on a hookah while sipping from the constant flow of mixed drinks coming my way. Every time my glass got down to half full it was filled up again. The experience reminded me of my family in Jordan and the summer I finally went to go visit them. The generosity. The dust. The place of my dad's birth. I let my mind drift.

I had been to Jordan once before when I was five but had little recollection of the trip. All I remember was a smelly camel ride and sitting on a lush carpet at my grandparents house eating Cheerios. Mom told me some stories that involved a family feud she witnessed resolved by two community elders dressed in cloaks wearing jeweled daggers at their hips. The rest of my memories are in the form of pictures in Dad's photo albums. Pictures of my grandmother wearing tribal paint on her face and my grandfather wearing traditional Bedouin garb. I always wished I had gotten to know them before they passed away.

Dad had been trying to get me to come visit Jordan for a long time and the timing finally worked out in August of 2007. I had close friends ask me why I wanted to go considering my strained relationship with my father. I'd tell them that no matter what had happened with Dad and Mom, I deserved to see where I came from.

My flight on Royal Jordanian Airlines took about 17 hours. I remember looking out at the glowing sunset over the Atlantic Ocean dreaming of Jordan. Dreaming of seeing my dad again.

My father and two uncles picked me up from the airport terminal in Amman.

"As-salam alaykum." Dad glowed when he saw his eldest son and gave me wet kisses on both cheeks and a long suffocating hug. He had greyed significantly since the last time I had seen him. He was an old man now.

"Alaykum salam." I said back wiping the saliva from my cheek with mixed emotions.

The rest of the drive to Madaba was narrated in Arabic. We drove nineteen miles south through the center of Jordan winding through tightly packed thoroughfares, traffic cirles, and erratic driving. From the car window I saw a man burning trash on the side of the road filling the air with a putrid smell. Behind the man stood a giant billboard paid for by the royal family. It said in both Arabic and English: *We look to a brighter future.*

We pulled up a side street and I deduced that we had arrived home. I saw no signs to indicate where we were though. It's not unordinary for streets in Jordan to be nameless. On this particular unnamed street, all five houses were owned exclusively by El-Tayyabs. To me it was El-Tayyab St. My aunt and uncles each owned a house on the street and lived there with their children and grandchildren. It was a multi-generational extended family living on the same unnamed road under adjacent roofs.

In the first house on El-Tayyab St. lived my dad's sister Roia and her kids Muhammad, Facep, Ahmed, and Hamnah. Next to Dad's house lived my uncle Hallad with his wife Selema and their six kids Faris, Feraz, Bedir, Abir, Adra, and Fahad. They also have six grand children. Next to Hallad lived my eldest Uncle Omar, his wife Fatima, and their eight children and three grand children Muhammad, Abdoula, Ahmed, Alia, Alla, Ruba, Ali, Naof, Sharif, Fatima, and Omar. The last house on the block is my dad's uncle Issa's home where he and his four children Muhammad, Ahmed, Isha, and Couter live.

I got out of the car with my luggage surrounded by family. *My* family. My long lost Bedouin tribe. Children ran around me and shrieked with laughter at me as they chased each other. With a hug and a kiss on either cheek my relatives embraced me, a family member they had missed for two decades. A family I had missed too.

I grabbed my luggage and walked down the stone path to my father's two-story home. His courtyard contained even more relatives conversing in Arabic, drinking tea, and smoking hookah.

"*Marhaba* Hassan. Welcome welcome." Uncle Omar greeted me with a wide grin and a firm handshake. "How's your mom? How is Sara?"

After many more hugs, kisses, and smiles food was served. Meals are the center of Arab life and my family is no exception. We sat down on my father's living room floor on a majestic carpet with blue and gold embroidery. My stepmother Sherifa placed a steaming tray of *magluba* in the center of the room. *Magluba* translates to mean "upside-down" in Arabic because the pot the rice and chicken is cooked in is literally dumped upside down on a large communal tray when it's served. Next she brought in plates of hummus and olive oil, plain yogurt, and piping hot pita bread. No plates, no spoons, no forks, or knives. Just bread and a massive tray of delicious *magluba*.

While we ate I observed how overwhelming it was to be in the presence of so many family members I didn't know yet who acted as if they knew me. I did my best to remember as many of their names as I could, accepting I'd fall short of learning them all.

*T*he next morning I awoke to the sound of a local Imam's call to morning prayer over a loud speaker at a nearby Mosque.

"Allahu akbar. Allahu akbar. Ashadu an la illaha illa allah." Bellowed the deep voice.

I rubbed my eyes from my spot on the floor of my dad's living room and saw on my watch that it was only 5am. The blue of dawn peeked in through the windows along with crisp morning air. My slumbering relatives near me barely stirred, impervious to the 5am alarm clock. I sat out on the steps of my father's house with a blanket observing the grape vines dangling around the yard listening to the morning prayer.

In the mood for exploring, I made my way down Dad's brick path barefoot only to be spotted from the street by a relative. Aunt Roia's son dragged me into their house and I was served Arabic mint tea. *Shwaya shwaya* or slowly slowly, they began to teach me a few words in Arabic. One of the more useful words I learned was *zaki* meaning delicious.

Later that morning Dad found me at Roia's house stuffed with Arab cookies, tea, and coffee. I asked him if we could go into Madaba for breakfast to see the ancient mosaics downtown that I'd read about. Dad agreed and asked my cousin Ahmed to warm up his bus, which he used to lead tours around Jordan.

I got on and sat in the front seat waiting for Dad feeling the rumble of the engine through the floor. More El-Tayyabs climbed aboard after me. Men in long white thopes, women in headscarves, and children wearing t-shirts and jeans packed in two to a seat. Pretty soon every seat on the bus was crammed with my relatives accompanying me for a trip downtown to get breakfast.

As we started moving my cousin Yousef grabbed the tour bus microphone and began singing a traditional Bedouin song.

Bela subu helgahuwa zidul hahel. Subu ana nashara ziduhahel.

Everyone on the bus started clapping and singing along grinning from ear to ear. I noticed two twenty-something men on a street corner clap and sing along as the bus rolled by. I joined in, doing my best to keep up with the Bedouin coffee song, fully caffeinated from my morning with Aunt Roia.

Yousef thrust the mic at me when they finished. "Hassan you are a musician. Sing an American song." He said in broken English.

"I'd rather hear your music!" I replied feeling put on the spot.

"Come on Hassan!" Yousef insisted and eventually dragged me to the front of the bus pushing the mic into my trembling hand. Wracking my brain for songs I thought of Ray Charles.

Hit the road jack and don't you come back no more no more no more no more.

My relatives clapped along smiling wide.

"Now you try." I instructed over the loud speaker.

Hit the road jack and don't you come back no more no more no more no more no more no more.

They sang with me trying their best to keep up while bellowing laughter. We finished singing the last line and they roared in approval. This moment led to a running joke the rest of my trip. Every so often my relatives would break out into *Hit the Road Jack* in varying degrees of English proficiency singing *No more no more no more no more no more* until we'd all burst into laughter again.

The trip that morning to get some breakfast at a shop twenty minutes away lasted for nearly four hours and took us through the heart of the ancient streets of Madaba. We passed a Christian Church covered in elaborate mosaics assembled during the time of Christ. Dad every so often would jump out of Ahmed's tour bus and say hi to random friends he recognized along the way making our progression nothing short of glacial.

Life in Jordan I learned has a much slower pace then I was used to in the United States. Long conversations, communal music in the form of singing and drumming, prayer, food, tea, coffee, laughter, and family were staples of everyday life. Life was built around these things. The beauty of Jordanian customs inspired me. Everyone was generous and opened their hearts to me in a very touching way. I had been taught to be ashamed of my heritage for so long in America but here I was, knee deep in a rich and beautiful culture with much still to learn and much to be proud of. For that I was grateful.

Later on in the week I took a road trip that spanned the vertical axis of the country. Dad insisted I drive. Dad, my cousins Farez, Ahmed, and I got into the four-door Toyota and we made our way south down the main highway in Jordan. We passed the Dead Sea and stopped for a salty buoyant swim. We continued on and further down the road the highway just ended. No sign, no detour, and no more road. It looked as if they were in the middle of construction on the southbound section. Dad made the call to cross the median and drive in oncoming traffic for a few miles till we were able to get back over. Luckily traffic was light.

Our second stop was the ancient city of Petra built by the Nabateans almost 2,000 years ago. Petra is a city carved out of mountain rock. Until the 1800s this city was a legend to Westerners till a European explorer disguised himself as a Bedouin and made his way down the two-mile Siq to the hidden city. We traversed the same two-mile long canyon littered with Roman ruins and ducts for running water.

After a while of walking in the shadows of the canyon, we came upon the renowned opening we had been searching for. I craned my neck to see the impressive Petra Treasury standing before us drenched in sunlight. The rose columns jutted high and flanked a dark rectangular opening in the mountain. Unlike what's depicted in *Indiana Jones and the Last Crusade* there is no Holy Grail labyrinth, just an empty room. The Petra Treasury's facade stands an impressive 82 feet wide and 128 feet tall. I had never seen anything as remarkable built by human hands in my life.

As I entered the clearing a multi-lingual Bedouin child sold me a post card with a picture of Petra and a poem from the 1800s.

> *It seems no work of Man's creative hand,*
> *by labour wrought as wavering fancy planned;*
> *But from the rock as if by magic grown,*
> *eternal, silent, beautiful, alone!*
> *Not virgin-white like that old Doric shrine,*
> *where erst Athena held her rites divine;*
> *Not saintly-grey, like many a minster fane,*
> *that crowns the hill and consecrates the plain;*
> *But rose-red as if the blush of dawn,*
> *that first beheld them were not yet withdrawn;*
> *The hues of youth upon a brow of woe,*
> *which Man deemed old two thousand years ago,*
> *match me such marvel save in Eastern clime,*
> *a rose-red city half as old as time.*
> *– Johann Ludwig Burckhardt*

We journeyed on and explored the tombs deeper into Petra. My cousins kept trying to convince me that we had seen the whole city about every half hour, but I had the map and knew better. Dad told me later that they were just tired of walking. I continued on alone, by foot.

At the very end of the city stood one last Roman building carved into a huge rock formation. Out of the corner of my eye I saw an arrow pointing to a small trail leading away from the structure and behind the mountain. It piqued my interest and I followed the conspicuous trail for almost a mile. The trail was a little treacherous, filled with loose stones and sharp inclines but I persisted. It looped around the mountain and ended at a small Bedouin dwelling carved in the rock. The owner of the house had flowers hanging up around his home which overlooked hundreds of miles of the rugged Wadi Rum Mountain Range. He noticed me and smiled. *"Marhaba. Inta kwayis?"*

"Marhaba. Amriki" I answered pointing to myself trying to explain to him I was American.

The kind Bedouin man offered me Arabic mint tea and I accepted. I sat on a boulder near his front door slurping as he offered to sell me artifacts that he claimed to have discovered in the tombs. I noticed a picture of King Hussein above his door. While we attempted to converse, my eyes took in the view over the brilliant mountain vista feeling an occasional gust of wind on my face from the neighboring valley. *Helua.* I thought. *Beautiful.*

I asked Dad later on in the trip if we could explore the Wadi Rum Mountain Range I had seen from the vista but he said no for a reason that surprised me: "If you see everything, you'll never come back to Jordan." He answered with sadness in his eyes. It made me sad too. I couldn't help but reflect on the heartache we had been through; me being raised without my father and him growing old without his son. It was my wish that Dad could let go of time lost but I doubt he ever will. Some wounds have a way of lingering for too long. Wadi Rum would just have to wait.

Chapter 27

"Through forgiveness, which essentially means recognizing the insubstantiality of the past and allowing the present moment to be as it is, the miracle of transformation happens not only within but also without." — Eckhart Tolle

Just beyond Muhammad's canopy, a white cloud of dust swirled outside engulfing the entire Playa, every pedestrian, and art installation along with it. It was the most intense whiteout yet. What awaited me in the dust that day? Some familiar energy drew me into the mystery. *Have I been here before?*

I picked myself up from the lounge and rode a communal Burning Man bike into the cloud. The wind whipped hard at my body nearly hurling me off the bike as I pedaled slowly through the loose sand. Dirt stung my eyes even with my goggles on.

Suddenly, I jammed on the brakes to avoid a most peculiar old woman in my path. She sat obscured in the whiteout as the dust swirled, unfazed by the wrath of the angry Playa gods. Her long silver hair was knotted into tight braids that fell down past her hunched back. Wrinkled skin hung off her face, but her eyes looked youthful. Youthful spirit or not, the image of an older woman on the ground in the dust storm concerned me.

"You okay? Do you need some water?" I asked her.

"No, no, I am quite alright, thank you. Please come sit next to me for a moment and keep me company."

"What are you doing out here?" I asked.

"Enjoying the dust. Offering Tarot readings to strangers in need." She deflected the conversation. "Care for a reading?"

"Sure." I wondered what she was thinking sitting out there in such a harsh environment experimenting with the Occult. I also wondered what her reading would tell me. I wasn't sure I even believed in the Tarot, but it intrigued me to have a chance to glimpse the future.

"Take the deck in your hand and shuffle. Think of a question you need answered." She passed me the deck and smiled at me as if we had been friends for ages. Her twinkling eyes were magnets for mine. "Ask it aloud in your mind and send your intention into the Tarot cards. When you are ready, spread them out and pick six cards."

I did as she asked and sifted the cards back and forth in my dusty palms. The winds raged, my thoughts searching for the most pertinent question to ask the Universe.

I spread the cards. Beautiful detail and bright color filled each one. She indicated the first card, titled The Moon. A woman with three faces, one pointing forward, one to her left, and one to her right. She wore a long white gown. Bright lights shone around her head. At her feet stood a three-headed lamb and in the corner a red crab.

"This first card in the series tells you how you feel about yourself now. You feel confused, vulnerable and full of doubts, however, all is not as it seems. Feel the fear and do it anyway, because all will turn out well. Embrace the new and unexpected in your life." She paused for a moment and observed me in the dust. "Your turbulent emotions are muddying the waters, so step back and try to find clarity of mind, although this may seem difficult. Things may seem tough or confusing but stick with it, it's right for you. The Moon is a good omen, remember." The woman spoke as if her words were truth. I didn't know what to think. Everything she said seemed to resonate though.

A moment that Maya and I shared rushed to the forefront of my mind. I pulled up to her place to drop her off after a huge fight and looked her in the eyes before she got out of the car. "I love you," I'd blurted for the first time. *Why was I so stupid?* The moment of vulnerability was met with a slammed car door. Thinking about the memory, made my head ache and I could feel my face become warm with shame.

The woman indicated the next card face up, The Devil. My heart sank a bit. Whatever she was going to say could not be good. On the card I saw a horned centaur in mid-dance, blowing a horn.

"This card in the series gives us insight into what you want most at this moment. The cards suggest that what you most want at this time you can't have, like the forbidden fruit, which makes it all the more tempting. Or you could go for it but you know that it would be a bad choice and for all the wrong reasons." She frowned as if she knew every mistake I had made with Maya. It almost scared me to hear her speak with such accuracy. "Yes, you want passion and gratification – just be careful where you go looking for it."

I remembered Maya walking onto her front porch after she left my car. The old wood planks creaked with each step. Roses clung to the white wooden lattice hunging from her porch roof, the flowers swaying a little in the late summer. Maya's blue eyes cut into me. *Why had I let her treat me like shit? Why did I crave connection with a woman so cruel to me?* My head throbbed harder. I massaged my temple. I was left with more questions than I had time to answer.

The woman pointed at the next card, "Judgment." An ancient Roman warrior stood with a red shawl over his left shoulder and winged helmet strapped to his head. His right hand held a burning torch coiled in snakes as the warrior looked down upon three mummies crawling out of opened caskets.

"This card gives us insights into your fears," she said. "You are afraid that the conclusions you've been wanting are delayed and fear any far-reaching changes ahead. Perhaps things aren't turning out quite as you expected for some reason – this is a period when your life will be changed dramatically. Fear not, although events will seem to be moving at a fast pace, any choice you make will change life for the better."

I thought of the choice to leave the East Coast on my road trip. I hoped it was the right choice. I thought of Boston and how my journey was not heading back that way for a long time. Boston and Maya were the past now. My family and friends were going to be far away as I began a new life out West. There was no going back. I choked on grit as a gust whipped. *What were the conclusions I was waiting for?*

The next card was Death. I felt a chill down my spine as I gazed upon the black-cloaked figure; the steep cliffs of Big Sur flashed in my mind. An iron helmet covered the being's head as it looked down at three naked maidens, each kneeling with her own unique offering for the dark figure.

"This card suggests what is passing for you. A time of absolute endings and brand new beginnings." Her voice quieted to a whisper and I leaned in to hear her over the raging windstorm. "Your life is going through a period of great transformation. Whilst it may be difficult or even painful, you will pull through. You will be free for a brand new phase in your life."

I heard the smooth jazz record that played as I fell in love with Maya. I thought of all the endings that would be met with new beginnings. Lara, her dog Huck, and a stark white apartment in Oakland. A new home far away from all the memories I had created for myself on the East Coast. A transition from that part of my story would be totally welcome. Both excitement and doubt filled my heart about all the unknowns that were just around the corner. There were bound to be some really lonely times ahead as I carved out a new life in the Bay Area, where my closest friend was a 37-foot metal bug. I was hopeful that there would be amazing times too.

The fifth card was The Hanged Man. A boney, thin man hung upside-down from a tree by his right foot. An eagle circled overhead, eyeing the man's plight below. Despair emanated from the image. "The Hanged Man represents everything that is going against you. You are allowing yourself to be emotionally victimized." She leaned in close and put her wrinkled hand on my shoulder. I felt her warm breath on my face as she spoke. "Don't try and hang onto someone for all the wrong reasons. Someone has to go, you must find the ability to let go and give this up. Don't worry. It will turn out for the better for you."

Maya's eyes shot at me like laser beams through the dust. I thought of the shame I carried since our relationship ended. I thought about how I was numbing myself from feeling anything with other women out of fear of getting hurt again. I thought about all the other parts of me that were numb most of the time too. *Why am I holding on to so much pain?*

She indicated the last card, The High Priestess, a pale woman dressed in a long flowing white gown. She stood at the bottom of a long stone stairway. The opening at the top of the stairs led to rolling green hills scattered with pine trees. She held an apple in her right hand and flowers in her left. Some of the petals were scattered at her feet.

"This card represents the outcome of your journey. Your intuitive powers are at their height at this moment in time. Only by listening carefully and trusting them completely can you embrace that power. Do this and you will make strong, clear, self-assured decisions. You'll be open to truth." She patted my hand and picked up the deck up off the desert floor.

"Truth," I repeated.

Dust continued to swirl and whip at both our bodies. A strong urge overcame me to ride off immediately. I suddenly knew what I needed to do at that moment. *Where was the Temple?* I peered into the dusty whiteout. I said my goodbyes to the woman and rode off with urgency contemplating all we had discussed.

Soon the wooden frame of the Temple came into view. The dust swirling around its lotus flower arches cast an otherworldly essence over the place.

I climbed up to the third floor and searched for a pen. I spotted one on the floor. Next to it sat a note: *I'll always love you. You would have been a great dad. It's not fair that you were taken from us like that. I'll do my best to raise our son. Love, Jane.* A picture carefully pinned next to it on the wooden railing of a beautiful family: a smiling mother, father, and son wearing whitewater-rafting gear. The three of them were superimposed over a steep rock face and a calm river that flowed the entire length of the photo. An inflatable raft and three sets of oars sat on the rocky shore waiting for them.

I could sense the energy of the Temple and the people around me. People sobbed and held each other. Others laughed. Some sat or stood in complete silence. I shared in the silence.

At my feet lay a black sharpie. I slowly picked it up and opened the cap. I touched the tip to see if there any ink remained, then found an empty space near the rail and wrote a name on the wood. Just a name.

I looked at the lettering of the word up close and then backed up to view it in the context of thousands of other messages awaiting their fate in the fire. The name seemed at home there among all the other stories.

Tear drops streaked through and blended with the playa dust on my cheeks. Part of me felt I should hide my crying. I looked around at the others in the sacred building and saw that many were crying too. We gave each other permission to be vulnerable.

In complete silence I made my way down the stairs, took another glance at the Temple, then turned my back to it. I pedaled on automatic pilot towards Deep Playa and the outskirts of the event's perimeter. I wanted to be alone. Winds raged as I fought to gain ground through the sandy abyss. My world was dust.

I came upon a woman seated in front of an old typewriter on a small stool. The woman was not startled by my quick arrival and remained focused on her writing amidst the windstorm. Her fingers popped the keys in quick bursts only stopping for an occasional moment of deep contemplation.

"Hello," I interrupted.

"Hello." She answered after a few seconds more of typing. "Just hold on for a while if you have time. I am writing a story for you." Her comment stopped me in my tracks and gave me a strange feeling. Everything rang with an odd familiarity. *What was she writing?*

Finally, she leaned forward, looking satisfied. "Done!" she announced. She handed me the note, jumped on her bike, and waved goodbye. Her figure only remained visible for a few feet before disappearing into the dust. All that remained was the desk and the note.

Hello Stranger,

To write the book that teaches you how to wake to the dream, you must become the wanderer, slow and deliberate. Your life must become the story that is the myth within the dream. There are no words on a page here, but a book holding the logos of your life.

"The logos of my life," I repeated aloud trying to piece together a meaning for myself, standing alone at the edge of the Deep Playa, choking on wind and dust, holding a scrap of paper. The words seemed like they held wisdom but something still was missing. I thought about the symbols of my life. I thought about my music, Maya, my mom, my cleft pallet, my dad. How did they connect? What was my dream? Not the phony dream I've been trained to want by corporations, school, the TV, radio, news, Republicans, Democrats, family, friends, and every song that's ever been written, but the real dream, outside every symbol that's ever been created. The dream beyond ego. Questions swirled like the clouds of white dust around me.

Chapter 28

"Just as a candle cannot burn without fire, men cannot live without a spiritual life." — Buddha

The crisp snap of night air woke me from my nap. I stepped out of my tent beneath stars hanging over Black Rock City and noticed the entire camp was deserted. It was almost time for The Man to burn.

I walked to the Esplanade and saw thousands of people gathered around the foot of the wooden base. A second perimeter of art cars gathered behind them. Multiple sources of music battled one another for listeners' ears. BOOM BOOM BOOM BOOM the dance music pounded. Colored blinking lights from every person and thing flashed and blinked with intensity.

In the middle of the commotion stood the event's effigy: The Man. His face, arms, and legs glowed bright neon yellow. His ribs lit in white.

Multicolored rockets shot from the solid wood base. The fireworks peppered the sky with loud booms. The crowd cheered wildly. I fought my way to the front through the masses, determined to reach the source.

A huge explosion suddenly rocked the ground, as the base of the structure lit up in flames. The Man was engulfed in a massive ball of fire. The shockwave threw back our bodies, blasting us with a moment of uncomfortable heat. Thousands of people tight to the perimeter pushed closer to the fire and squeezed in as near as the intense heat would allow. The Man was finally on fire.

"BURN HIM DOWN! TORCH HIM!" Voices shouted all around me.

Hot smoke billowed and swirled in the evening wind over the loud crackling of burning timber. The night air was saturated with the scent of scorched wood and ash. I half wanted to pull myself away from the intense heat and thick smoke, but stayed to absorb every last bit of the experience.

After about an hour of burning, every bit of wood plank had been reduced to a carbon gas, except for the Y frame and the Man, which still stood, refusing to be beaten by the fire.

"This is taking forever," complained the guy next to me. The crowd murmured impatiently.

I looked up at the smoldering structure in the center of thousands of aggravated onlookers. We had to surrender though. We had no control. *Or did we?*

I went for a walk as the Y frame continued to smolder. I cut back through the dense crowd, dodging the first perimeter of stationary art cars, scanning for familiar faces. Nearby, I saw some folks from the Department of Spontaneous Combustion. A line of custom-built trikes spanned the horizon. Each trike held a long propane torch, illuminating the surrounding area. I saw that Don and Rebecca sat on one.

"Hey guys. Does it always take this long for The Man to burn?" I asked.

"It'll happen. Don't worry. Swig while you wait?" Don offered. His white beard hung several inches below his chin and tapered to a point.

The fiery liquid tingled on its way down my throat.

"Since we have the time, pull this lever," Don suggested.

I tugged on the thin wooden handle. A huge ball of flame shot out of the trike's poofer, and I heard gasps from several passersby. Some of them stopped and basked in the warmth. I gave another tug and heard cheers from below.

"I want to see this Man burned already," I commented.

Don chuckled. "You might have to burn your expectations first. Do that and things can be wondrous." *Wondrous.*

I got the sudden urge to head back to the still-burning Man, hanging on to his tired Y frame. Thousands of people remained, waiting for the collapse of the tenacious structure.

As I walked, I saw a group of seven people carrying a large wooden building frame. The four by fours wobbled at the corner brackets as the group pushed forward with their heavy burden.

"LITTLE HELP PLEASE!" The man in front called as the team clung on to their end of the oversized frame as they weaved through the crowd.

I jumped in and grabbed a corner, not entirely sure where they were going, or what was going to happen.

"OUT OF THE WAY!" We yelled as we made our way through the throngs.

The crowds finally broke apart and we found ourselves in front of a sea of red and orange embers. I squinted involuntarily and sweat trickled down my face; I forced an inhalation out of necessity, struggling to draw the hot air into my lungs.

"One, two, three," chanted the guy at the front, and we launched the object at the base of the Man. The impact sent the last remnants of the sculpture tumbling to the ground. Sparks and coals flew into the air as the crowd erupted all around us.

"WHOOOOOOOOOOOOOOOOOOOOOO!!!" thousands screamed.

Burners descended on the circle of embers, venturing as close as they could. A few people stripped and ran around the red-hot coals, weaving in and out of the onlookers. I suddenly had the urge to strip too, but then rethought the idea. It would take me a few more years of coming here before I was *that* open.

We began to circle the glowing rocks, as if instinctually reaching for an ancient part of ourselves.

I observed a nude woman kneeling before the glowing embers. She was covered in tattoos, beautiful drawings that accented the long lean lines of her body. Her breasts pressed against the earth, and her dreadlocked hair accented with a wreath of leaves. She seemed to belong there, rooted to the ground, her diaphragm expanding and contracting with the natural rhythms of the Playa. After a final backwards glance at one of the sexiest women I had ever seen, I moved away from the crowd and the fire with pangs of longing.

I broke free of the crowd and found myself completely disoriented. The Man had been a navigation beacon from anywhere on the Playa. Now were forced to find our own way. The vacant space reminded me of what Don had just told me. *Burn your expectations.*

Thousands of dusty bodies streamed away from the glowing circle of rocks. All of them with their own wants and desires. All of them with their own vibrational frequency attempting to get in line with those wants and desires. All of them doing their best to let go of their resistance to the current; to let go of the fear, the doubt, the unworthiness and to be carried down the stream to the higher version of themself. Toward the place inside our heart we call home.

I stood and absorbed the heat. My heart began pounding, pulsing warm blood through my veins. *I'm going to burn my next song.* I could hear a faint guitar melody hum in my ear, growing steadily clearer amidst the chaos.

Chapter 29

"The grand show is eternal. It is always sunrise somewhere;
the dew is never dried all at once; a shower is forever falling;
vapor is ever rising. Eternal sunrise, eternal dawn and gloaming,
on sea and continents and islands, each in its turn,
as the round earth rolls." —John Muir

After a few hours of perusing the night scene and illuminated art structures, I found an art car with a spinning teacup attached to its back trailer. The art car was actually a white truck with gold stripes painted along the sides. A ladder behind the cab led to the mouth of the teacup, which was also rimmed with gold.

"Hey, mind if I go for a ride?" I called to the driver over the hum of the idling engine.

A wooly bearded guy in a tiger costume peered down at me. "Sure, jump on."

Three people were already seated inside. As we careened through the night, we rotated the steering wheel at the tea cup's center as fast as we could. The neon lights of the city spun and blurred into a long strip of multicolored glow. When we finally screeched to a halt, the guy across from me turned green.

We turned down a shadowy side road lined with vehicles and shade structures. I recognized my surroundings - we had driven through the Nine O'clock Plaza to the edge of the city.

"Everyone out," called a voice from the cab of the teacup as we pulled to a stop. I jumped off the back of the truck and landed with a thud. A cloud of dust rose up ankle high. It was well into the early morning hours, and quiet had settled over the Playa.

I strolled alone down a side street lit enough by the moon to see my surroundings. A huge metal horse sat tucked away among the tents lining the road, its face illuminated by strings of orange and green light. I walked up and inspected the metal work, something I had found myself doing since I'd joined the Fishbug crew.

Suddenly, a girl tapped my arm and I jumped.

"I didn't see you there!" I said catching my breath. I noticed the girl's bright blonde hair strung in braids flowing over an acoustic guitar strap slung over her shoulder.

"Sorry about that. Did you make this?" She ran a hand over the coarse steel. "Hey, look over here." She wandered further into the campsite.

The horse art car was attached to a Conestoga wagon. The wagon was stuffed with turntables, PA speakers, and sub woofers. All essential items for a Conestoga wagon to carry.

She started walking and motioned for me to join her.

"I'm Evol," she stated proudly. "Evolution and love."

"You play that guitar?" I asked.

"I do. I'm a songwriter."

"Cool. I write songs too. Or, I used to write songs anyway. I've been in a dry spell."

"We've all been there. How long's it been for you?"

"Too long," I answered heavily.

"People didn't always have the entire burden of creative output on their shoulders you know. The ancient Greeks used the idea of a genius to account for inspiration. A genius was a deity that lived inside every object and helped direct and guide your life." Evol gave me a warm empathetic smile. "Every artist had one who guided his or her creative process. If you think about it right, a genius could really take the pressure off. That means no one is a genius, they just *have* a genius."

"I like that!" I could tell Evol had fought with writer's block before and won.

Our conversation flowed as we walked. Soon we found ourselves close to the gentle curves of Fishbug. I could see a corner of sun poking up over the horizon. The orange glow brought a flicker of warmth to our cold bodies.

Evol gazed at the sculpture as we came in closer. "This is awesome. How did I miss it?"

Evol peered over my shoulder. "What is that?" She pointed to a peculiar object in the ground inside Fishbug. Welded to three crooked legs was a cylinder with a round plastic face, blinking a soft blue light in steady rhythm. I walked over and picked up both the tripod and the note it stood on.

"Can you read the note aloud?" She set down the tripod and began a series of yoga poses and stretches. Her hands pressed against the soft sand and she lifted her left leg back behind her.

Dear YOU,

I needed to find a home for this Tripod. It told me it likes the chaos of chance, and wanted to be left here to be found by YOU. Please take care of it and give it a name. Part of taking care of the Tripod is making sure that it gets back to the Burn each year. Only during this week can the Tripod be close enough to talk with its brothers and sisters, so please do your best to get it back here. Be good to the Tripod and it will be good to you.

The secret of the Eye:

After the Burn, the light will fade as the Tripod goes to sleep. The first Tripod told me that if someone made a wish while that Eye was lit, it would come true after the light faded out. I'm a big skeptic when it comes to this stuff, but the Tripod told me: "One man's Magic is another man's engineering. Supernatural is a null word." I asked it to explain further and I have to admit, its reasoning made a lot of sense.

So in short, thank you for taking care of this Tripod. I am sure it has found a great home.

Sincerely,

LostMachine

PS- I think the Tripods met Heinlein

The Man from Mars Robert H

"Great find!" exclaimed Evol. "Who is Heinlein?"

"Heinlein is a Sci-Fi writer." I passed her the note. "I like his quote about, 'specialization is for insects.' "

"What are you going to name it?" she inquired.

"I don't know. Maybe Merlin," I answered without thinking.

"How about Warlock?" She laughed. "It looks like a Warlock to me. The note said he was magic too. That's my vote."

"Maybe Merlock?"

"I like it." She nodded. "Yeah, that's his name." I looked away, distracted by the sunrise over the Temple.

*E*vol and I stepped outside Fishbug's belly to witness the dawn unfolding like a movie. The sun hovered next to the Temple across the Playa. Later that day it would burn just as The Man had the night before. But this burn would feel differently. For this burn would contain the shrines of 50,000 people. I thought about my wish Merlock owed me. *Merlock, help me fix the hole in my heart with my next song.*

I looked on with awe as the glowing orange ball blasted light over the mountains, diluting the dark blue of the night sky. Others had stopped in their tracks to appreciate the temple sunrise too.

Chapter 30

"What is commonly called "falling in love" is in most cases an intensification of egoic wanting and needing. You become addicted to another person, or rather to your image of that person. It has nothing to do with true love, which contains no wanting whatsoever." — Eckhart Tolle

I woke up later that morning with images of The Man burn, a metal tripod, a girl named Evol, and a scarlet sunrise attached to a wish burned into my memory.

After breakfast, I threw my water bottle into my backpack, and prepared for my next adventure. By that point, I was on exploration autopilot. I ended up at the intersection of Nine O'clock and DNA and saw an interesting building covered in fake jungle foliage. I heard acoustic music playing from within.

Inside I found two guitar players and a percussionist playing *Scarlet Begonia* by the Grateful Dead. We all sang the lyrics:

As I was walkin round grosvenor square
Not a chill to the winter but a nip to the air,
From the other direction, she was calling my eye,
It could be an illusion, but I might as well try, might as well try.

At a lull in the sing along, I was startled to find myself on the receiving end of a gentle kiss. My cheek burned. Sunlight poured in from behind her. She snapped a photo of me. "HASSAN! We met at Jenee's house warming party in Boston a few months ago."

"Gretjen of course! I remember. What are the chances?"

"I found you because of your music. We are going to Heebeejeebies now, if you want to join my cousin Jenny and me. It's a little further up here. The talk is about relationships."

*T*he three of us arrived at a tan colored shade structure soon after. People stood around the canopy, poking their noses through the seams of the fabric, trying to get a look at the source of the calm voice amplified through the PA.

The speaker was a bald man in his early 40s with white bushy eyebrows perched above a pair of round glasses. He wore a white shirt that fit him loosely and red silk pants embroidered with images of finely woven leaves and flowers.

"Childhood dramas mark the beginning of our adult dramas." He spoke calmly into the microphone. "People's issues are derived from these events, sometimes even beyond the scope of our memories. They have powerful implications. We can stay in these cycles our entire lives, cycles that stem from a brief period in our pasts. Awareness and the opening of hearts are important in breaking these cycles and understanding them for what they are."

He pointed across the tent. "Question in the back."

A man stood up. "I feel as though there are games you are forced to play in relationships. Do they tie into the notion of childhood drama?" He paused a moment to collect himself. "What is your response to this need to play games, and are they necessary?"

The speaker looked thoughtful. "I will begin by saying that the truly authentic person will not be drawn to things of this nature. They are aware of the roles and prevent negative cycles before they start."

I leaned forward and tried to determine which category my relationships fell into.

He continued: "People can get trapped into different roles in relationships before they have truly dealt with these dramas. A game can start when two people recognize each other in opposite roles. The victim will try to get others to do something for them rather than doing it themselves. Somewhere along the line, they have convinced themselves that they are not capable of coping on their own. A rescuer will try to make things easier for the other person, thus giving them a position of power in the relationship. It might make them feel as though they have the upper hand and it may fill them with a notion of purpose."

Several people shifted uncomfortably in the warm tent. I found myself shifting too.

I heard my doorbell ring at Dustin street and opened it to see Maya, a week after she came up with the idea to break off our relationship. Her bloodshot blue eyes wet with tears. I reached out held her in my arms and she wept harder. *I don't want you to hurt.* She kissed me on my neck. "Can I come in?" We lay on my bed and she eagerly took off her clothes. I opened my still-wounded heart so she could feel less alone for a moment.

The speaker stepped forward and began speaking in a softer timbre. "But why do people get into these patterns and what holds us there? An authentic relationship where two people simply relate to each other can be a scary thing. Many people put their energy into the games and scenarios that I have described as a way to subconsciously protect themselves for various reasons. Again, this often stems from the childhood dramas I spoke of earlier, where there has been neglect, abuse, faulty role modeling, and so on."

An incomplete memory from when I was 4 came to me. My body suddenly began to sweat, as if my body was wringing out my subconscious mind like a soaked sponge. I was napping with the light on in my room, my body wrapped tightly in a thick white comforter. Outside a commotion. I saw the profile of my dad standing in front of my mother. Shouting, crying, more shouting. My heart pounded in my chest and I pulled the covers over my head.

"DARBA FI' ALBAK!" I heard my dad scream before a loud smack.

"STOP YOUSEF!" Mom screamed.

I winced at the impact and began to cry hot tears. My hands gripped a toy dog I had found under the covers. I scratched behind its plastic ear as if he were alive and in need of attention. The toy was in my hand for a moment and then it was gone. Buried in an avalanche of sheets. I patted the mattress from under the blankets trying to find the toy. The screams in the other room became muffled in the background of my rescue effort. All I knew was I had to find the dog. Where did it go? I checked in the pillows, under the bed, under the mattress but no use. I never did find it. The rest of the memory is blank.

The speaker paused and looked around the room, his eyes meeting mine briefly. "How does one break these patterns? First it is wise to figure out what role you find yourself getting into the most frequently. Are you the Victim, the Rescuer, or the Persecutor?"

I thought of the day we left Dad. The day we stopped being a family. The day that opened a hole in my heart. I thought of how brave my mom was running with the fear that Dad might have killed her if he caught her in the act. Her love was big enough to wrap around the whole world. My mother risked everything. She truly saved my sister and me. She's the bravest woman I'd ever met. She broke the pattern, I realized suddenly almost breathless if she could break her pattern, so could I. *Mom's been a rescuer my whole life. Did she teach me to be a rescuer?*

As I processed this, the words came into focus. I noticed the speaker glance at the clock. "Once you recognize these roles, you can spot them as the relationship is beginning to form. If you are self-aware, you can better control your behavior patterns. Another thing you might try is to take a positive attribute found in your 'role' and use that small part at your own discretion and in a controlled way. If you are the rescuer, use the resourcefulness you have but remember to give sparingly. Being conscious of all these roles will really be the way to break unhealthy relationship habits and cycles. Recognize other people's inner child as their own. There is nothing to take personally. So that is about all the time we have for the moment. Thank you all for coming today. Namaste."

"What's your name?" a voice called.

"It doesn't matter who I am." He smiled politely. "Thank you all for coming. I'd love to stay and answer more questions but a yoga class is about to start very soon, so enjoy the rest of your day."

I stretched my back and neck as people began to get up to file out. The talk felt like an emotional work out. It made me realize how much personal work I still needed to do to understand some of the traumatic things I'd been through. Getting more guidance with these complicated emotions might be exactly what I needed.

Jenny leaned forward to join the conversation. "I liked his suggestion that you ask your partner to play an active role and help you through things, rather than approaching a situation from the roles you are both used to playing."

"Right, just point it out as it occurs." Gretjen nodded. "It's a bit of tough love."

Jenny looked thoughtful. "You have to avoid giving in to empathy and keep in mind what you really want."

"Maybe that is an act of empathy?" I noted.

The three of us stepped out into a patch of warm sun. A juggler walked by, clubs spinning end over end. "Where are you guys off to now?" I asked.

"We're going back to our camp to get ready for tonight. Why don't we meet up later?" They turned to walk away, and Gretjen called back over her shoulder. "Look for an Alaskan flag hanging from the door."

I walked away from the girls and one thing kept coming to mind. A thought that rang clear as a bell. Something I could say every day for the rest of my life. *Thank you mom. Thank you mom. Thank you mom.*

Chapter 31

"Where there is love there is life." — Mahatma Gandhi

At about three fingers, I left camp to find an Alaskan flag attached to an RV. My bike squeaked down Kinship Street, towards the outskirts of the city. Beyond was open playa.

After a lengthy search, I knocked on an RV door that fit the girls' description. Jenny answered.

"Hey, come in." She tipped her cowboy hat to greet me. "We're almost ready to leave. Have a seat."

"Quick, close all the windows!" Gretjen pointed at the growing dust cloud headed for the RV.

Once the windows were secure, everyone took a seat again at the table. "Many people are leaving today, and are kicking up a lot of dust, but it is too hot to keep the windows closed. We are just making do," Jenny commented.

After a few moments, Gretjen appeared, her long, dark, curly hair brushed down her shoulders. A faded white shirt with a watermelon design peeked out from under a long barreled camera hanging from her neck. "Ready to go," she announced.

The three of us stepped outside and were joined by Gretjen's friend, Jason. Neither Jenny nor Gretjen had bikes of their own, so Jenny jumped on my handlebars and Gretjen jumped on Jason's.

Jenny gripped the handlebars tight. It was slow going at first, but it got easier once we were moving. People tended to clear out of our way when we yelled that we couldn't stop.

Center camp traffic was thick and slow moving. People packed in almost shoulder-to-shoulder. It became too hard to steer with Jenny on the handlebars so we decided to walk. Gretjen and Jason rode ahead not noticing we weren't keeping up.

"Let's keep going." Jenny seemed totally at ease with the turn of events. "Maybe we'll run into them later."

We walked further and came to an art installation at the plaza just outside of Center Camp. All week I'd seen people climbing the metal structure. Jenny was determined to get to the top of the swinging metal butterfly and I followed.

The butterfly grew out of a gigantic metal flower that spun like a mobile. Solid footholds allowed us to climb to the top of the forty-foot metal frame. I watched Jenny clamber up the sculpture until her short skirt and bright red stockings were all that were visible.

I got to the top of the structure slightly out of breath. As we looked out, it felt like Jenny and I stood at the border of land and sky. Everyone below us looked like colorfully costumed ants wandering through the Black Rock City. The setting sun splashed brilliant oranges and reds that blended into the streaks of clouds all around us. With a twinkle in her eyes, Jenny pretended to grab a chunk of the sky and put it in her bag.

"What did you think of that talk today?" Jenny asked me from her perch on the spinning flower.

"It was interesting for sure." I said, gripping the rail.

"I thought so too." She paused. "I'm in a thing with someone now and… I dunno. He just doesn't have the energy for the relationship that I do. It's become a bit of a one-sided infatuation."

"How so?" I asked, feeling my stomach tighten a bit. Just hearing that got me thinking of my unhealthy infatuation with Maya.

"He's a total free spirit. I kept writing in my journal, 'Jenny, he is just a symbol' but I don't know." She looked sad and turned away towards the fading sun. She signaled to me she wanted to get down off the sculpture. We climbed down in silence.

"It's funny how we can project our wants onto other people." I commented, breaking the stillness as our feet met the hard packed sand.

Jenny nodded. "It was like he represented my ideal self. But he didn't have the energy for the relationship. I guess I ride on a pretty high energy level for all of my relationships." She giggled. "Maybe in the same way I'm a bit swept by him, I might sweep others." I looked at Jenny staring off at the Temple. My heart started to beat a little faster as I regarded her graceful outline. I wondered how she saw me in that moment.

"I probably need to be more cautious in the way I am perceived. The love I give the world is both impersonal and personal."

"Personal and impersonal?" I asked.

"There's a place you get to when you feel comfortable enough around someone to be your authentic self. At that point, I feel impersonal love. I am grateful for the space to be myself. But at the same time, it's not that I love the person, though they might take it personally."

"We all want connection. No shame in that." I said.

"And to love big is to feel pain." she said with heaviness in her expression.

"Love big," I repeated with a similar sadness noticing the quickening fade to night sky.

Her eyes met mine and she smiled. "Love in itself is such a pure thing, but think what comes from it: hate, impatience, jealousy, anger, fear, and so on. It enables us to have our shit come up to be dealt with. Hopefully at that point you learn more about yourself and possibly heal."

"You are letting yourself be seen." I glanced across the Playa as the sun finally dipped below the mountains. The glow of small lanterns began to flicker along the main road as the parade of ceremonial lamplighters lit the path to the Temple. There was only an hour or so left till the burn.

"The beauty and the ugliness," she said, leaning heavily on the last word. In her I saw the former.

Somewhat appropriately the next sculpture we came across was a blown up heart. The plastic exterior had been painted dark red with blue veins running down its side. Hollow arterial branches protruded from the top and sides of the plastic shell. Ladders hung off the side branches.

She quickly scaled up the ladder disappearing into the arterial tunnel, while I sat down on a random couch for a quick breather. I took a big swig from my water bottle as she explored the heart.

Jenny came down the ladder and sat down next to me, out of breath.

"Wow, this couch is comfortable. Wish we could sit on this at the Temple burn."

"Maybe we could," I said jokingly.

"Maybe you're right!" Her eyes lit up. "We could just carry it."

"Ummm, I don't know if that's such a good idea." I estimated the distance across the Playa to the Temple from where we stood and concluded that it was FAR.

"Sure it is. It's a great idea!" she exclaimed.

I finished stalling and finally gave in to her plan against my better judgment. "Alright," I grumbled.

I took the front of the couch and she grabbed the back. Together we lifted.

"Damn, this is fucking heavy," I blurted out.

"Yeah I know, but we got this," she assured me.

Step by step we walked the couch across the Playa toward the temple, stopping every once in a while to rest, complain, or laugh. After about forty-five minutes or so, we were finally at the Temple.

A ranger along the perimeter called to us as we plodded by. I knew he was there because the crew had begun loading the Temple up with explosives for the burn ceremony. We set the couch down and listened.

"Hey, what are you guys planning on doing with that couch?"

"Well, we were going to sit on it and watch the burn," I answered as if this were rational behavior.

"I hope you two will bring it back where you found it. Why don't you set it down that way a little bit." He pointed us further back from the sculpture. "Don't put it too close to the perimeter; you don't want to block anyone's view."

"No problem," Jenny answered, winking at me covertly.

We walked the couch a little further back and set it down with a heavy thump. She gave me a high five.

"Nice work," she said.

I sat down on the couch and rubbed my sore shoulders. She sat down next to me under my arm and snuggled up close. "You're warm." She began to purr and nuzzle in close. It felt good to have her next to me.

Stars began to flicker overhead when the temple ceremony began. In less than an hour our perch was surrounded by thousands of people and art cars. A few other folks sat down on and around our couch, forming a little living room out there on the Playa.

Past the caution tape, fire dancers began to perform in front of the temple. The flames whipped around their bodies in graceful and flawless motions.

The Temple's lotus flower timbers curved elegantly into the night sky while its base, set with intricate wooden inlays, stood solid on the desert floor. All the detailed work that had taken who knew how long to assemble was about to be torched in a matter of moments. The fire spinners backed away from the structure and the Temple was engulfed in flames. Crackling and popping could be heard as wafts of smoke filled the night air above the burning shrine.

"It's beautiful," Jenny whispered, still clinging to me for warmth. I nodded in agreement eyeing her looking at the burning Temple. She was beautiful too. Her eyes were just so curious and alive. It felt amazing to have this wonderful woman so close to me. My heart began to race as I acknowledged my attraction to her. If hearts have doors, mine opened a crack.

Staring at the inferno, I thought of the name I had written on the Temple. A name that had sent me on a trip of a lifetime that had tested every ounce of my being. For the first time in a long time, I felt ready to let go. I was ready to embrace someone new. I was ready to fill this hole in my heart with rain pouring in it. I was on the path I needed to be on out here in the wilderness of my emotions and what I really needed to do was just let go. Just like this temple, things come and go and you have to move on.

My thoughts of Maya kept swirling like the smoke billowing from the burning Temple. Our paths had brought us together for a short while only to pull us apart in the end. Lessons abounded from that haphazard summer love affair and I felt ready to learn from them.

*M*y arm pulled Jenny in closer. My body ached for her. There was nowhere else on Earth I would have rather been at that moment and there was nowhere else on Earth I should have been.

I looked again at the fire and saw Maya's blue eyes staring back at me. A strong gust of wind, and she was gone. An illusion; a moment in time that had ended. Why did I care still? None of this was about Maya at all. I looked deeper into the flame. I could make out an image, but it was still hard to see.

The fire raged intensely. Timbers fell with a crash, sending hot coals into the air. The blurry image became one. I thought of my father. I thought of the last conversation Dad and I had face to face, almost a year ago. I felt every memory I had of him broken open staring at the fire: broken hearts, broken promises, broken vows, and broken memories. So many sad thoughts. The smoke from the Temple billowed harder.

I gazed at my dad's face in the fire with careful detail. I saw his greying hair, and black and silver mustache. The lines in his cheeks made him look like an old man. I was older too, older than he when he first met my mom. I observed his shaded aviator prescriptions glasses that hid his eyes. I looked past the lens, and saw his glass eye being forged in heat.

"Dad." I had paused before continuing, afraid of my

question. "What happened to your eye?" I had always wondered how he had lost his eye, but never asked outright. Maybe I thought asking him would make the pain of losing the eye physically hurt again. Maybe I was afraid to know. A long silence followed. I let him speak first.

"I've never told you? I guess you've never asked."

I shook my head. Mom thought for most of their marriage that he lost it to glass shards from a car accident. My uncles had told me another story. There were so many unanswered questions I didn't know what to believe.

Dad rubbed the lid under his glass eye almost instinctually. I could see his whole body sink deeper into his armchair. "I was about fifteen or sixteen. I had some problems at school and my teacher spoke with my father. Your grandfather was furious with me. He took off his shoe and threw it accidentally hitting my eye. No one took me to the doctor for a few days but by that time, it was too late."

"I'm... so sorry Dad." A wall from the fiery sanctuary crashed to the ground, and woke me from my thoughts. I could feel my stomach tighten as a wave of burning heat washed over Jenny and me.

"It's ok. I can still see with one eye." Dad blinked his good eye and smiled. I looked at his glass eye closely for the first time. The skin sagged around it making him look tired. The glossy painted iris of the ball colored a slightly different shade of brown from his right eye.

"Are you mad at your dad for hurting you?"

Dad leaned forward in his chair and gave me a serious look that gave me a chill. "Hassan, he asked the doctor if he could trade his eye for mine. The technology." He stumbled on the word. "Technology, how you say it? Technology wasn't good enough. I went to Germany for the surgery. Pressure, pressure, throbbing pressure all the time. I'd have to go to bed by 4 every day. Hassan I swear to you, it hurt so badly. The doctor said he needed to take the eye or it would keep hurting."

My eye hurt hearing him speak. I thought of everything that he had to endure. I thought of everything Mom, Sara, and I had to endure. I felt like crying as I stared at the flames.

"Why Germany?"

"There were better doctors there. And I was shy. Shy, shy. I couldn't talk to girls. No confidence."

I recognized he said shy, but it seemed like he meant ashamed. Ashamed of loosing his eye; of being disfigured. Had he ever stopped running? Was I running by leaving Boston?

"But I'm a man Hassan. I don't care what anyone thinks."

"You had to leave your home? I'm so sorry, Dad." I thought about him moving to Germany with no family or friends. He was just a kid.

"Yes. I dropped out of high school and left. I couldn't go back. I got there in the middle of winter and slept on the streets of Berlin for eleven days. I've done it all, Hassan!" He bellowed with pride. "If there is a feeling good or bad, I've felt it."

I had wanted to ask more questions but everything seemed clear. *Clearer* anyway. I thought about everything that had happened to our family. *Was this the beginning of it all?* The beginning of our suffering as a family. The beginning of him abusing my mom; beginning of the fights, the divorce, the gambling, us running out of a hotel room in terror; the beginning of me growing up without a dad around; the beginning of giving away my heart for free to people that didn't deserve it; the beginning of my trip out here into the desert, my trip to Burning Man. My dad has had a harder life than most people I knew. He had lost everything. Though nothing could make what he did ok, I saw him through the eyes of an adult for the first time because I was an adult now. I had the choice to not be a victim anymore. His eye was part of his burden. My scar was part of mine. I was beginning to understand the struggles that connected us.

I stared at the intense fire scorching the burning temple. The vision of my father disappeared. The sacred building had almost completely transformed into ash, smoke, and a bed of hot coals. I pulled Jenny closer. Her body felt warm. My burden seemed lighter. So did my spirit.

"Goodbye's too good a word," I said aloud.

"So I just say fare-thee-well," Jenny replied pulling in closer.

Upturned faces all around me were held in unique poses, some crying, some laughing, and some in complete silence. I shared in the silence, totally overwhelmed by the power of the moment. What an amazing place. Here we were, people from every corner of the planet, sharing a profoundly spiritual experience together. Not one wrapped in dogma, but in a collective need for community and self-healing.

"We have to get this couch back to the heart sculpture," Jenny said as she extracted herself from my lap. The crowds around us began to dissipate, some drifting towards the smoldering embers.

I groaned sarcastically. "Don't remind me."

We both stood and stretched in preparation for the long trek back with the couch.

Jenny got a mischievous look in her eye and approached a cluster of people who were still milling.

"Who wants to help us carry this couch? I know you want to," she coaxed.

In a matter of moments she had organized a group of ten strangers to help carry an oversized piece of furniture they had no allegiance to across a vast expanse of Playa to an undetermined location.

"Everyone grab a side," she directed.

Thanks to Jenny's recruits, we got the couch back to its original resting place with minimum effort. It weighed almost nothing divided among all of us.

Jenny and I walked back toward the fully lit Fishbug, not far from the heart.

She smiled at me. "That was fun."

I smiled back, sad that the night was ending. "Yeah, it was."

She gave me a long hug under the stars and walked away into the darkness. I felt a pang of longing as I watched her go.

Incredible woman. I wondered if what I had experienced was the impersonal version of her love. I could see that a lot of guys might take her openness the wrong way. I would be lying if I said I didn't wish things went further that evening. I guess I could have tried to make something happen, but for some reason, the evening felt complete in the way it ended. What love she did give me, personal or impersonal, I was able to genuinely receive and felt worthy of receiving. Not only that, I felt like I was a little closer to giving it back too. Experiences like that were what I really needed right now, as I was about to head to the East Bay to rebuild my life. As Jenny walked away, I felt a deep longing, but the kind of longing that makes you feel alive.

Chapter 32

"The best way out is always through." — Robert Frost

I woke up the next morning with a song stuck in my head and the image of the Temple burn flashing behind my eyes. Burning Man was over and people were beginning to head back to their respective parts of the planet. I was heading back to the East Bay to share an apartment with my new roommate Lara and her dog Huck. So much had happened that week, and much of it was still processing in my mind.

People all around me were busily packing up their belongings. The RV next door had already moved out and the tents across the way were gone. The people on my left were struggling to take down a giant parachute.

I sat in front of my tent holding my acoustic guitar as the city disassembled before my eyes. Dropping the guitar into an open C6 tuning, I rested my fingers on the cool steel strings of the instrument. Something inside me felt different. My thoughts seemed quieter. I took a deep breath and began a finger picking pattern in a steady rhythm. It started with a riff and the melody slowly evolved. The image of the Temple burn was in my mind's eye. A good hour or two must have passed, but before I knew it, I had a complete instrumental song.

It was a songwriter's dream come true. I couldn't remember the last time I'd finished a song all at once. The last chord rang out and negative thoughts started jumping up, but I intentionally blocked them from my mind and stopped them from picking at the integrity of the new born creation. The song was done, and the only thing to do at the moment was let the moment be.

The image I had in my head of going back to the East Bay with no new song faded. I was heading back there with new music. New original music that sounded beautiful even to critical old me. It felt amazing to have this little gem of a tune I could share with people, because in the end, music is really meant for sharing.

"Temple Sunrise," I said aloud when I was done playing. That's what this one is called.

*L*ater that morning I headed out to help break down Fishbug for load-out. "Hey, Hassan. Can you take the propane lines off the manifold?" Rebecca was fiddling with an impact driver when I arrived. "It takes a 9/16ths wrench."

The End and Beginning
Afterward

"Nice take, man. I think that was it," James called from the control room of the recording studio.

"Yeah, that felt pretty good," I said, setting my guitar back on the stand and taking off my headphones. I flicked my guitar strings and they rang out in its open C6 tuning. The condenser microphone stared back at me but didn't look as intimidating as it once had sitting perched on the black boom stand. The track, Temple Sunrise, only needed fiddle and electric guitar and it would be ready for mixing.

Almost a year had gone by since my first visit to Burning Man. Here I was, still in the East Bay, trying to finish my new band American Nomad's debut EP. Though it was A LOT of work wrangling eight professional musicians, it felt great to be performing with amazing players and moving forward with the music. It felt good to even have a band name finally. I had been trying to figure that one out for quite a while.

On another musical side note, that October after Burning Man, I got hired by a nine-piece jazz swing ensemble called the Megaflame Big Band as a lead guitar player. My first gig in San Francisco was in front of 600 people!

That year I continued to learn about metal from Jess and Rebecca, and really from anyone who had the time to show me. I spent a lot of time at the Shipyard working on the gasifiers with Jay and the rest of the folks at All Power labs. I also took some classes at a local vocational college to get more in depth welding training. By February, I got a job as a metal worker for some artists in Emeryville.

When I have a spare moment I work alongside Rebecca and Jess who still make incredible art and bring it to huge festivals around the West Coast and beyond. We did a few more shows with Fishbug that fall in LA and around the Bay Area, and even built a set of eight flame cannons for a Phish concert in Coachella Valley. Jess and Rebecca, along with many other talented folks, created a non-profit called the Flux Foundation to continue their mission to form and teach communities of people around building large art. Through a series of coincidences, they were asked to build the Temple for Burning Man in 2010, which they agreed to, and so appropriately named it the Temple of Flux.

So much changed in my year of flux in the East Bay that it's hard to recount everything. Of course things were difficult, like they usually are when you are adjusting to such drastic changes, but it was a good difficult. The kind of difficult that makes a person grow. I can say that it would have been a lot harder if I didn't have some great folks helping me along the way. Thank you to Mom, my sister Sara, Sarah Rabe, Hope Rideout, Lyric Cox, Star Simpson, Rebecca Anders, Jess Hobbs, Gary Gregory, Cheryl Fralick, and the rest of the Fishbug crew, Jim Mason, Jay, Bear, and the rest of the hard working folks at All power labs, the Flux Foundation, Lara and Huck, metal artists Peter Neufeld and associates, Meagan Rutigliano Angela Laflame and the rest of the Megaflame Bigband, Olinde Mandel, Mark Lipman, Mike Daillak, Ben Andrews, Will Rzad, Mary Redente, Justin Purtill, to James Rowlands our recording and mixing engineer, to Dana White for mastering, Ryan Lukas, Erik Yates, Matt Crimp, Mikiya Matsuda, Adam Lowdermilk, Brian Judd, Jan Purat, Maren Metke, the T Sisters, my Producer Laurie Lewis, and Amal Dar Aziz.

Thanks to all the Kickstarter folks for contributing to the financing of this project. Lastly Thanks to the amazing community of people whose efforts combine to create one of the coolest annual events on earth... Burning Man.

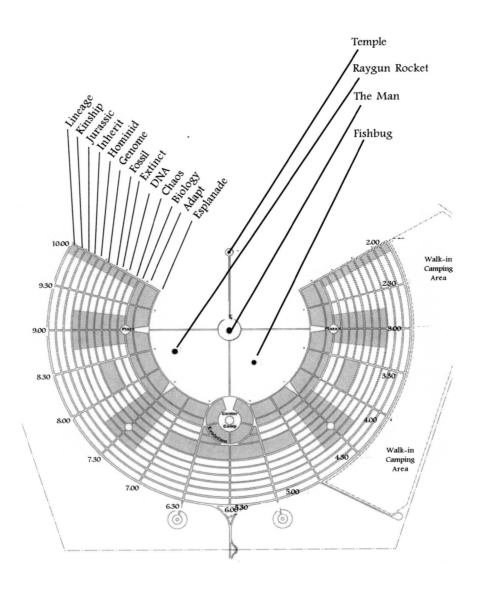

Black Rock City
2009

Temple Sunrise

Hassan El-Tayyab

Biography

*H*assan El-Tayyab is an award-winning singer/songwriter, author, teacher, and cultural activist currently residing in San Francisco, California. His critically-acclaimed Americana act *American Nomad* performs regularly at festivals and venues up and down the West Coast and beyond. In addition to performing Hassan is also a music educator, having taught songwriting and guitar classes for the *Freight and Salvage* and *The East Bay Center for the Performing Arts*. Hassan has also been a guest lecturer on song writing at the University of California, Berkeley. You can follow Hassan and his music at www.americannomadmusic.com.

CPSIA information can be obtained at www.ICGtesting.com
Printed in the USA
LVOW10s0222070116

469167LV00005B/8/P